University Futures, Library Futures

Aligning library strategies with institutional directions

Constance Malpas, Roger Schonfeld,
Rona Stein, Lorcan Dempsey, and
Deanna Marcum

ITHAKA S+R

University Futures, Library Futures: Aligning library strategies with institutional directions

Constance Malpas

Strategic Intelligence Manager and Research Scientist, OCLC

Roger Schonfeld

Director, Library and Scholarly Communication Program, Ithaka S+R

Rona Stein

Researcher, OCLC

Lorcan Dempsey

Vice President, Membership and Research, and OCLC Chief Strategist

Deanna Marcum

Senior Advisor, Ithaka S+R

October 2018

OCLC Research
Dublin, Ohio 43017 USA
www.oclc.org

ISBN: 978-1-55653-076-0
DOI: 10.25333/WS5K-DD86
OCLC Control Number: 1056765822

ORCID iDs
Constance Malpas: iD http://orcid.org/0000-0002-9312-8294
Roger Schonfeld: iD http://orcid.org/0000-0003-3047-0858
Rona Stein: iD http://orcid.org/0000-0002-9862-6655
Lorcan Dempsey: iD http://orcid.org/0000-0002-2925-8764
Deanna Marcum: iD http://orcid.org/0000-0002-4345-952x

Please direct correspondence to:
OCLC Research
oclcresearch@oclc.org

Suggested citation:
Malpas, Constance, Roger Schonfeld, Rona Stein, Lorcan Dempsey, and Deanna Marcum. *University Futures, Library Futures: Aligning Library Strategies with Institutional Directions*. Dublin, OH: OCLC Research.
https://doi.org/10.25333/WS5K-DD86.

Contents

Figures

Chapter 1: Project History, Background, and Objectives

The University Futures, Library Futures project grew out of a conversation between Lorcan Dempsey and Deanna Marcum observing that OCLC Research and Ithaka S+R have a long-standing, shared interest in the evolution of academic libraries. Both organizations have a distinctive "system-wide" perspective on changes in the higher education sector, as those changes are reflected in choices about (and investment in) library services and perceptions of library value.

This perspective is a useful complement to institution-scale, practitioner-oriented research on academic libraries and disciplinary research in library science. They reasoned that their two organizations might productively join forces to carry out a collaborative project on the future of academic libraries. In particular, they share a belief that the future of academic libraries can only be understood in the context of changes in the higher education landscape. So we wanted to embed a discussion of libraries very much in an analysis of the shaping influence of higher education.

We approached The Andrew W. Mellon Foundation to see if there might be interest in supporting this collaborative research project, and we were encouraged by Senior Program Director Donald Waters to develop a proposal. Each organization conducted preliminary background research before we met to begin developing the outline of the project.

Higher education is in a pivotal moment. The history of increases in student enrollment since World War II is well documented, and the nature of changes in enrollment patterns was very interesting to us. Enrollment in degree-granting institutions increased by 15% between 1992 and 2002. Between 2002 and 2012, enrollment increased 24%, from 16.6 million to 20.6 million. Much of the growth between 2002 and 2012 was in full-time enrollment; the number of full-time students rose 28%, while the number of part-time students rose 19% (National Center for Education Statistics, 2015).

At the same time, higher education is now the subject of an intense debate about mission, organization, and direction. This is driven by multiple factors, including affordability and inclusion, research evaluation and the associated influence of rankings, and increased recognition of the diversification of mission. An important strand in the US has been the discussion about institutional isomorphism, which has featured centrally in influential recent contributions.[1] Institutional isomorphism refers to the tendency of institutions in a field to come to resemble each other over time, shaped by coercive (mandated) or normative (professional) influences. In the higher education field, Michael Crow and William Dabars have coined the terms "Harvardization" or "Berkeley envy" for a historical trend they observe: universities have aspired to those institutions as common models of excellence.[2] They, and others, argue that the needs of their constituencies demand a more plural form of education, where different types of institutions fit different niches.

And, indeed, we have observed in our own work how universities are sorting themselves into new patterns of development. For example, Crow's own institution, Arizona State University, is very deliberately charting a course as a new type of mega-university, arguing that it is possible to increase simultaneously both inclusiveness and research excellence. Other patterns are apparent: the residential liberal arts college, for example, which is developing career-oriented professional online offerings (e.g., Indiana Wesleyan University), the regional public university seeking to streamline based on a distinctive career focus (e.g., the University of Texas Rio Grande Valley), the system with shared services (e.g., University of Georgia), and so on.

We wanted to know if library services are changing in response to the changes in institutions of higher learning.[3] Since the explosion of growth in higher education in the 1950s and following, libraries of all types have followed essentially the same pattern: they measured their effectiveness by the size of the collection. In the mid-1970s, Evan Farber, a prominent thinker on academic libraries, deplored this tendency to view library value in terms of collection size as "university-library syndrome," arguing that individual libraries should instead tailor their offering to the specific curricular needs of the parent institution.[4] The impetus to count the number of volumes available to students on the campus grew out of the notion that students would have access to information that the library acquired and preserved. Until recently, the collections model of libraries has meant that all academic libraries have measured their success in terms of how big their collections are—every library trying to be as much like Harvard as possible.[5] The Association of Research Libraries annual statistics reinforced the notion that the biggest collection was the best, and smaller libraries imitated the process to determine which medium-sized or small library is "best."

But libraries are not ends in themselves. They serve the communities and organizations of which they are a part—they serve the interests of their parent universities and colleges.

As we note in a recent research article, "the most important long-term influence on the library is the requirement placed on it by changing patterns of research and learning. These changing patterns... are shaped by the focus of the parent university or college and the directions it is taking."[6] Network and digital technologies have changed dramatically the ways in which researchers and learners create, share and employ information resources. The library can no longer define its quality in terms of collection size; services are the new differentiating factor. Our research question, then, is: what happens when libraries differentiate themselves in terms of services, not collection size; are there multiple models of success?

Our working assumption was that colleges and universities do, and will increasingly, attempt to differentiate themselves to succeed in a highly competitive market. We further hypothesize that academic library services may benefit from—and some indeed are already benefiting from—undergoing a disruption to allow them to adapt to rapid changes in academic institutions' business models and value propositions. We contend that the most important long-term influence on the library is the requirement placed on it by changing patterns of research and learning. These changing patterns, in turn, are shaped by the focus of the parent university or college and the directions it is taking.[7] And, as we noted above, a variety of patterns is emerging here.

Second, it often presumes some homogeneity of approach or direction, different only in degree among libraries. This presumption of homogeneity encourages a view of academic libraries in which the research library is seen as a terminal point in evolution, rather than as one type among others. However, where universities and colleges seek to differentiate themselves this presumption is increasingly misleading. The models of excellence for libraries supporting, say, an elite comprehensive research university, a liberal arts college devoted to broad-based student learning, or an increasingly career-oriented public institution will be very different from each other.

These factors mean that despite considerable exploration, discussion of library futures can be somewhat partial. We contend that different types of academic libraries will be on different vectors, influenced by the increasingly different needs of the types of universities or colleges they support.

Our work has three main components, and while we cooperated across the range of work, each partner had some lead responsibilities. OCLC Research led on developing the first component, a working model of US higher education institutions, while Ithaka S+R led on developing the second, a library services framework. The third component involved comparing the two to test our hypothesis that the services portfolio of libraries will map onto the institutional priorities of their host university.

In the first component, we aimed to develop institutional typologies that provide a more nuanced description of institutional characteristics than the commonly used "basic" Carnegie Classification. In our project, we combined elements of the more robust Carnegie classification by selectively incorporating the same underpinning statistical indicators into a simpler framework. The team also incorporated the Integrated Postsecondary Education Data System (IPEDS) 2015 institutional survey data into the formulation of typologies. This led to a model in which university emphases can be characterized in two dimensions. The first is educational activity, and here we characterize an institution in relation to its distance from three poles: research, liberal education, and career-directed educational programs. This captures the "what" of what institutions offer. The second is mode of provision. Here we define two modes: a traditional-residential mode, and a new-traditional-flexible (or convenience) mode. This captures the "how" and the "for whom" of what institutions offer.

The second component developed a framework of library services, and then explored patterns of adoption of those services through a survey of university libraries.

The team developed a framework of library services models to help explore patterns that are emerging in different institutional settings. We reviewed the websites and planning documents from dozens of academic libraries selected at random from across the higher education landscape, and iteratively developed a services framework. We reviewed the framework with a variety of library leaders, and we revised the framework to include nine key areas:

- Convene Campus Community: Provide spaces and facilitate programs for the community broadly or specific subpopulations to generate engagement, outreach, and inclusion.

- Enable Academic Success: Support instruction, facilitate learning, improve information literacy, and/or maximize retention, progression, graduation, and later life success.

- Facilitate Information Access: Enable discovery and usage of information resources of any format or ownership; provide for preservation of general collections.

- Foster Scholarship and Creation: Deliver expertise, assistance, tools, and services that support research and creative work.

- Include and Support Off-Campus Users: Provide equitable access for part-time students, distance and online learners, and other principally off-campus/non-campus/remote users.

- Preserve and Promote Unique Collections: Ensure the long-term stewardship of rare materials and special collections, and maximize their usage.

- Provide Study Space: Provide physical spaces for academic collaboration, quiet study, and technology-enhanced instruction and/or learning.

- Showcase Scholarly Expertise: Promote research excellence and subject matter expertise of scholars and other affiliates; includes repository activities for open access preprint materials.

- Transform Scholarly Publishing: Drive toward modernized formats, revamped business models, and reduced market concentration.

We explored how important these services areas were to library directors now, and we asked how important each should be as the library met institutional priorities.

Finally, the third component of our work tested our hypothesis by comparing the outputs of the first two components to see if libraries were in fact adapting to fit the institutional priorities of their institutions.

For example, we hypothesized that a research library will have strong incentives to provide support for emerging forms of digital scholarship, and to provide curatorial services for a broad range of research outputs. A library in a teaching-focused institution may invest more in services supporting areas relating to student success. Some libraries will assume responsibility for the print scholarly record; others will gradually divest. Likewise, the sourcing of core services will vary: some will be internalized and promoted as institutional differentiators; others may be externalized to third parties (including commercial vendors, consortial providers, or cooperative/shared services arrangements).

The research presented in this report supports a number of important and interesting conclusions. We call out a few of these here:

- Our research has validated the importance of institutional directions in shaping, if not determining, academic library services directions. A deeper understanding of emerging institution types, supported by the framework developed in this project, is helpful to academic library directors for services planning, benchmarking, and identifying institutional partners for collaborative projects.

- To explore current and future service directions in academic libraries, we found it useful to abstract a small number of key services areas, within which individual library activity and investments may vary. This enabled us to compare current and future library resource allocation in different institution types, and examine where patterns of investment converge or diverge. A notable finding is a shared desire among academic libraries to reduce allocations to Facilitate Information Access in favor of other areas. This finding is consistent with a growing body of evidence suggesting a shift in focus from collections management to engagement-oriented services.

- While the growing focus on career-directed learning and changing demographics of higher education are familiar themes in the literature of higher education policy and administration, they are less often a focus of attention in library administration or planning. An important contribution of this work has been to focus on the role of libraries in supporting university goals around preparing students for careers, as well as supporting New Traditional students.

The chapters that follow provide detailed descriptions of the research and the findings. The aspiration for this project is that libraries, as they shift their focus from building collections to developing responsive services, will find it useful to place their institutions into the multi-dimensional typologies we have developed and configure services that best meet the needs of their particular students and faculty.

Chapter 2: Literature Review

The literature review underpinning our institution typology was undertaken to assist in identifying institutional characteristics that are not sufficiently addressed in existing classification schemes. Our review focused on recent research literature on the US higher education system, with a particular emphasis on drivers of institutional change with respect to the scope of educational offerings, and the demographics of student enrollment.

On systems of classification in US higher education

WHAT IS CLASSIFICATION?

Classification is an omnipresent human activity, an organizing principle, an important aspect of how we perceive and make sense of the world. Higher education institutions (HEI) in the US have been characterized in a variety of ways. A common characterization distinguishes between "elite," "mass," and "universal" systems of higher education.[8] Other characterizations identify higher education systems on either "vertical" or "horizontal" dimensions, with the former staggering institutions according to their reputation, status, and prestige (e.g., "world class"), and the latter emphasizing more functional differences between institutions (e.g., "entrepreneurial").[9]

There is ongoing debate about the appropriate unit of analysis for understanding higher education processes and activities. Some researchers argue that the primary object of interest is not the individual college or university but rather at the micro level—departments, faculties, research centers, and even individual scholars—or, at the macro level—the entire national higher education system.[10]

The differentiation of higher education systems and institutions is the outcome of the relationship and interaction between these units.

Existing approaches to classifying higher education institutions

The need to classify institutions to "appropriately describe and compare those that are sufficiently similar"[11] has generated numerous detailed taxonomies, two of which are widely employed and both are based on data from IPEDS, which is collected by the US Department of Education's National Center for Education Statistics (NCES).

THE NCES SURVEY OF INSTITUTIONAL CHARACTERISTICS

The NCES prepares this taxonomy by cutting data on postsecondary institutions by several institutional characteristics, most notably sector, which is derived through crossing control of institution (public, nonprofit, or for-profit) and four-year or above, two-year, or less-than-two-year (i.e., public four-year or above, nonprofit four-year or above, for-profit four-year or above, public two-year, nonprofit two-year, for-profit two-year, public less-than-two-year, nonprofit less-than-two-year, for-profit less-than-two-year). While effective for years, concerns have been raised about whether this approach is still adequate for today's policy and practices, which increasingly blur the lines between institutions, given that this approach tends to mix institutions whose mission is exclusively focused on bachelor's programs and above, with those that are predominantly focused on associate's degrees and vocational programs but which offer one or two bachelor's degrees.[12]

THE CARNEGIE CLASSIFICATION

The Carnegie Classification represents the most extensive, empirically based, and time-tested taxonomy for postsecondary education to date.[13] Published in 1973 by the Carnegie Commission on Higher Education and its parent organization The Carnegie Foundation for the Advancement of Teaching, the widely used Carnegie Classification of degree-granting US colleges and universities was initially developed to support the commission's program of research and policy analysis.[14] "The Carnegie Classification utilizes survey data from the Department of Education's IPEDS, the National Science Foundation, The College Board, and the 1994 Higher Education Directory published by Higher Education Publications Inc. (HEP)."[15]

According to the basic framework of the Carnegie Classification,[16] *Doctoral Universities* include institutions that awarded at least 20 research or scholarship doctoral degrees during the update year (excluding professional practice doctoral-level degrees, such as the JD, MD, PharmD, etc.) by an aggregate level of their research activity (highest, higher, or moderate).

Master's Colleges and Universities include institutions that awarded at least 50 master's degrees and fewer than 20 doctoral degrees during the update year and are regarded according to their size (larger, medium, or smaller).

Baccalaureate Colleges Include institutions where baccalaureate or higher degrees represent at least 50%of all degrees but where fewer than 50 master's degrees or 20 doctoral degrees were awarded during the update year; these are divided into arts and sciences focus, and diverse fields.

Baccalaureate/Associate's Colleges include four-year colleges that conferred more than 50%of degrees at the associate's level and are divided into mixed Baccalaureate/ Associate and Associate's dominant.

Associate's Colleges include institutions at which the highest-level degree awarded is an associate's degree. The institutions are sorted into nine categories based on the intersection of two factors: disciplinary focus (transfer, career and technical, or mixed) and dominant student type (traditional, non-traditional, or mixed).

Special Focus Institutions include Institutions where a high concentration of degrees is in a single field or set of related fields.

Tribal Colleges are colleges and universities that are members of the American Indian Higher Education Consortium, as identified in IPEDS Institutional Characteristics.

Currently, the Carnegie Classifications offer six categorizations of US colleges and universities: Basic, Undergraduate and Graduate Instructional Program, Enrollment Profile and Undergraduate Profile, and Size and Setting.[17] As Prescott points out,

"the fact that the Carnegie Classifications encompass so many different approaches is testament to the fact that the post-secondary education industry in the U.S. resists a single, or even simple, approach to categorization."[18]

A brief historical context to the Carnegie Classification

Before 1960, higher education in the US was a loosely organized institutional field.[19] The Carnegie Classification was developed at a time when complexity and change in US HEI were at an all-time peak. The number of colleges and universities grew rapidly over the preceding century, with only 250 schools at the time of the Civil War to about ten times that number by 1970.[20] The number of students enrolled in postsecondary institutions in the US tripled between 1950 and 1970 from three million to nine million.[21] In just the ten years leading up to the activity of the commission that created the Carnegie Classification, the academic profession as much as doubled its size (260,000 faculty members in 1960 compared to 530,000 in 1970, including 383,000 full-time instructors).[22]

The US higher education system was shaped by cultural change, as well as demographic shifts. While 19th and 20th century students were relatively cloistered from broader societal developments, the social movements of the 1960s and the decline of *in loco parentis* norms resulted in far more permeable organizational boundaries,[23] through which social issues percolated into HEI and vice versa. Coursework and academic units in the social sciences, natural sciences, and applied fields proliferated, altering the traditional focus on humanities as the academic core of higher education. Changes in admissions policy contributed to the development of a more diverse student body, in terms of gender, ethnicity, and socioeconomic class, in both public and private institutions.[24]

As the scale of the higher education enterprise grew, institutional differentiation increased, as did the need for an apparatus for organizing, understanding, and assessing colleges and universities. "It was during this period that the shape of institutions began to change dramatically. For the first time in American higher education history it was necessary to construct a taxonomy that described the varying range of institutional types."[25]

Limitations of the Carnegie Classification

In the four and a half decades since the Carnegie Classification was first published, the US higher education system has continued to evolve, and the Carnegie Foundation has produced increasingly nuanced extensions to the original classification. The most recent update of 2015 represents the seventh version of the original schema and features 33 categories in its "basic" classification.[26]

While widely used, the Carnegie Classification is recognized as having some flaws. One line of criticism points to the idea that the *a priori* approach of the Carnegie Classification is based on a set of mutually exclusive categories, rather than allowing the categories to emerge from the data. This top-down approach is said to be particularly inadequate for capturing new or emerging organizational forms (e.g., alternative medical schools, distance learning colleges, etc.). Furthermore, as organizational sociologist Steven Brint observes, "a difficulty of all a priori forms of classifications is that they are ultimately based on informed intuitions about meaningful differences" which may or may not accurately represent the affinities or differences among institutions.[27]

In other aspects of criticism, scholars have argued that developing more and more detailed classifications does not necessarily provide additional help in understanding the structure of higher education.[28] A third critical point observes that the clear boundaries of mutually exclusive categories do not lend themselves well to the often fuzzy and partial membership in categories, which has been recently recognized in organizational studies.[29] Lastly, it has been argued that ranking systems marginalize classification systems. Catering to the competitive traits of high-status institutions, high-achieving students, and their parents, ranking systems have generally assumed greater prominence than classification systems, at least in the public sphere.[30]

In light of these claims, there is a need for classifications that do not simply reinforce the view that "elite" and highly selective institutions are the highest form of educational success, but acknowledge the distinctive capacities of more inclusive institutions that nonetheless excel at retaining and graduating students with qualifications suited to a range of professional pathways.

On the evolving student profile

The demographic profile of students enrolled in US colleges and universities has evolved over time, following broader demographic shifts in the population, as well as changes in the labor market. In this section, we explore these changes as reflected in statistical data on students' age, gender, ethnicity, socioeconomic class, and full-time compared to part-time enrollment in degree-granting postsecondary institutions. There is increasing attention in research and higher education policy to how colleges and universities are responding to these changes, from a pedagogical and curricular perspective, as well as a student support services perspective.

Our analysis here focuses on changes in the balance of "traditional" (full-time, residential) and "non-traditional" (part-time, adult, and historically underserved communities) enrollment in four year colleges and universities. We favor the term "new traditional" over "non-traditional," as the latter suggests an ahistorical conception of the "normal" enrollment pipeline and student experience. As defined in the research literature,

New Traditional learners have at least one of the following attributes: they have no high school diploma, are enrolled more than one year after high school, are financially independent from parents, work full-time, or are responsible for children or other dependents.

In addition to these student groups, we might add the overlapping populations from the bottom quartile of income, immigrants, and first-generation college students, who have trouble succeeding in college because of lack of comfort, lack of money, or both.[31] Highlighted below are some of the prominent shifts in student population in recent decades.

AGE

While most college students have been, and are still, 18- to 24-year-olds, data show that the 1980s and 1990s saw increased cohorts of students entering higher education in the age groups of 25 and older, and 35 and older. After peaking in 1990, these trends have endured over time and are projected to carry on in the next decade, as seen in figure 1.

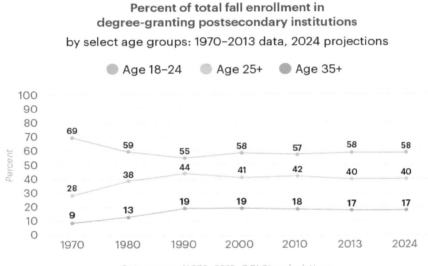

**Percent of total fall enrollment in
degree-granting postsecondary institutions**
by select age groups: 1970–2013 data, 2024 projections

● Age 18–24   ● Age 25+   ● Age 35+

Figure 1. Percent of total fall enrollment in degree-granting postsecondary institutions, by select age groups: 1970-2013 data, 2024 projections.

As shown in figure 1, 18- to 24-year-olds accounted for 69% of the total enrollment in degree-granting postsecondary institutions in 1970, while older students, ages 25 and older, accounted for only 28%.[32] In the next two decades, however, decreased percentages of 18- to 24-year-olds were enrolled in higher education (55% in 1990), relative to enrollees age 25 and older (44% in 1990) or age 35 and older (19% in 1990). Neither 2013 data nor 2024 projections show significant changes (2013 data: 58% age 18–24, 40% age 25 and older, 17% age 35 and older; 2024 projections: 58% age 18–24, 40% age 25 and older, 17% age 35 and older)[33]

GENDER

In 1869-70, women comprised only 21%[34] of the total fall enrollment. Their percentage rose only modestly over time and by 1950, women still accounted for only 30% of students. Since 1980, however, women have been enrolling in higher education in increasingly larger numbers than men: 51% women compared to 49% men in 1980, 56% women compared to 44% men in 2000, 57% women compared to 44% men in 2014, and this trend is projected to slightly increase to 59% women compared to 43% men in 2025[35] (2014 and 2025 percentages are rounded, therefore they seem to exceed 100%). These data are depicted in figure 2.

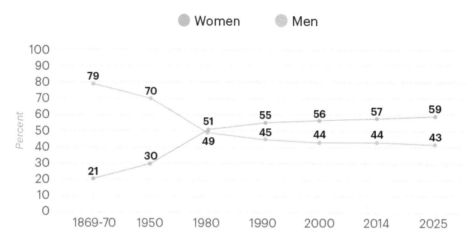

Percent of total fall enrollment in degree-granting postsecondary institutions by gender: 1869–70 to 2014 data, 2025 projections

Data source: NCES, 2016a, 2016b, OCLC's calculations.

Figure 2. Total fall enrollment in degree-granting postsecondary institutions, by gender: 1869-70 to 2014 data, 2025 projections.

As of 1970, women age 35 were enrolling in higher education in small numbers, as were same age group men (5% women, 4% men), but over time women age 35 and older have been enrolling in higher education institutions in close to double the percentages as the same age group of men,[36] as seen in figure 3.

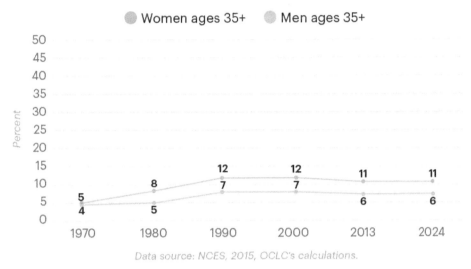

Percent of total fall enrollment of students age 35 and older in degree-granting postsecondary institutions

by attendance gender: 1970–2013 data, 2025 projections

Figure 3. Total fall enrollment of students age 35 and over in degree-granting postsecondary institutions, by attendance gender: 1970-2013 data, 2025.

As shown in figure 3, by 1980, women age 35 and older enrolled in close to double the numbers as men in the same age group (8% women, 5% men in 1980)—a trend that has been kept relatively steady through 2013 (11% women, 6% men) and is projected to go on (11% women, 6% men in 2024) .[37]

ETHNICITY

The share of 18- to 24-year olds who enrolled in higher education has been greater among White students compared to Black and Hispanic students, as seen in figure 4.[38] While increasing shares of 18-24-year-olds in these three ethnicity groups have risen, a gap of roughly 8% remains between Black and Hispanic enrollment compared to White enrollment. Additionally, the gap between Black and Hispanic enrollment, which has persisted for decades, closed in 2013.

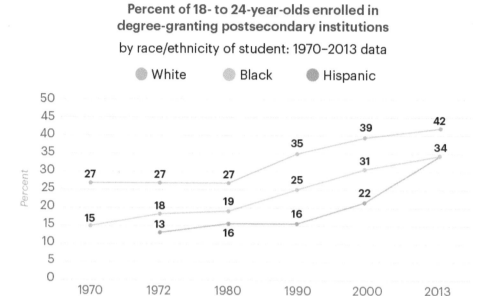

Percent of 18- to 24-year-olds enrolled in
degree-granting postsecondary institutions
by race/ethnicity of student: 1970–2013 data

Data source: NCES, 2015a.

Figure 4. Percentage of 18- to 24-year-olds enrolled in degree-granting postsecondary institutions, by race/ethnicity of student: 1970-2013.

In 1970, 27% of the population of White 18- to 24-year-olds in the US were enrolled in degree-granting postsecondary institutions, compared with 15.5% of same age Black population. Hispanic student enrollment was first reported in 1972 to be 13% of the population of this age group, compared to 27% White and 19% Black).[39] The decade 1980 to 1990 saw an increase of White and Black enrollment (35%, 25%, respectively in 1990) and the succeeding decade saw another increase, this time including Hispanic enrollment (39% White, 31% Black, 22% Hispanic in 2000). The most recent available data from 2014 show a modest increase in White and Black enrollment (42% White, 34% Black) and a bigger increase (34%) in Hispanic enrollment. These data show that young adults in all three major ethnic groups are enrolling in greater percentages in HEI.

SOCIO-ECONOMIC CLASS

In the last four decades, there has been a 20% to 30% increase in the number of recent high school completers who enrolled in two-year and four-year colleges in all family income levels, as seen in figure 5.

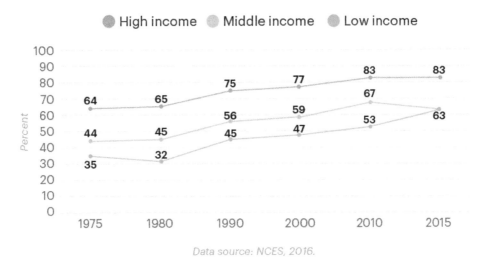

**Percent of recent high school completers
enrolled in two-year and four-year colleges**

by family income level: 1975–2015

● High income ● Middle income ● Low income

Figure 5. Percentage of recent high school completers enrolled in 2-year and 4-year colleges, by family income level: 1975-2015.

While higher percentages of recent high school completers in all family income levels have been enrolling in two-year and four-year colleges in the last four decades, there are clear differences between enrollees from low, middle, and high family income (low refers to the bottom 20% of all family income, high refers to the top 20% of all family income, and middle refers to the 60% in between).[40] The highest percentages of college enrollees come from high-income families (64% in 1975 to 83% in 2015), compared to enrollees from low-income families (35% in 1975 to 63% in 2015). Recent high school completers from middle-income families have been enrolling at percentages higher than in low-income families but still not as high as in high-income families (44% in 1975 to 63% in 2015). As the data in figure 5 show, the gap between enrollment percentages in low and middle family income, which had persisted for years, closed in 2015, rendering the data consistent with other findings that demonstrate a hollowing out of the American middle class.[41]

PART-TIME VERSUS FULL-TIME ENROLLMENT

The share of full-time enrollment always has been greater than part-time enrollment, but part-time enrollment increased sharply between 1970 and 1990, going from 32% to 43%, while full-time enrollment decreased during those years from 68% to 57%, as depicted in figure 6. Since 2000 there has been a modest increase in full-time enrollment compared to part-time enrollment—a trend that is projected to continue in 2024 (full-time 62% in 2013 and 2024 compared to part-time 38% in the same years).[42]

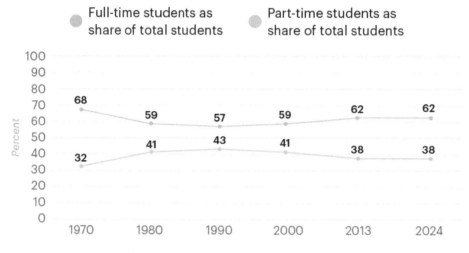

Percent of full-time and part-time enrollment of total fall enrollment in degree-granting postsecondary institutions

1970–2013 data, 2024 projections

Data source: NCES, 2015b, OCLC's calculations.

Figure 6. Share of full-time and part-time enrollment of total fall enrollment in degree-granting postsecondary institution: 1970-2013 data, 2024 projections.

As shown in figure 7, the share of women as part of total enrollment, as well as part of full-time and part-time enrollment has risen over time (women comprised of 41% to 57% of all enrollees in 1970 through 2013, 44% to 59% of all part-time enrollees, and 40% to 55% of all full-time enrollees in the same years, with these trends projected to continue into the next decade.[43]

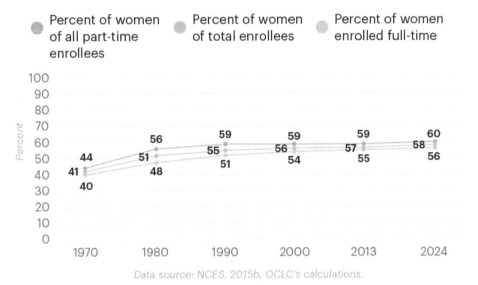

Figure 7. Percent of women as part of total enrollment, full-time enrollment, and part-time enrollment of the total fall enrollment in degree-granting postsecondary institutions: 1970-2013 data, 2024 projections.

Given that roughly four in ten students are enrolled part time (as seen in figure 7), and that roughly six in ten part-time enrollees are women, it is apparent that part-time enrollment is particularly prevalent among women.

NEW-TRADITIONAL STUDENT PROFILE

The historically typical profile of the financially privileged, young, White male student has evidently transformed as reflected in the enrollment trends shown and described above. Furthermore, with today's—and tomorrow's—labor market's greater opportunities for college educated workers, both the supply of and demand for higher education have skyrocketed. The US Department of Education traced these same trends and projected that they would persist through 2025 (the last year for which projections were made in this report).[44]

Over time, increased diversity within the enrollment pipeline will result in a rebalancing of the student profile. As Van der Werf and Sabatier observe: "[a]t some point, probably just after 2020, minority students will outnumber whites on college campuses for the first time."[45] Additionally, Van der Werf and Sabatier predict that, due to stiff competition, the colleges of the future will tap into segments of the population that include, in their words "high-school dropouts, first-generation students, and adults who need retraining in their present career, for an alternate career, or for a first career." Retirees could also be a segment of the population who might seek higher education, not necessarily for career training but rather for leisure and enrichment.[46]

Toward a new typology of higher education institutions

Educational directions

In broad strokes, the educational activity of colleges and universities focuses on three areas: Research, Liberal Education, and Career-directed Education, as defined below. Importantly, these areas are not mutually exclusive, meaning higher education institutions are likely to engage to varying degrees in all three of them. In practice, this could mean different organizational units (i.e., departments and schools) and/or levels (i.e., undergraduate and graduate) focus more or exclusively on one area, while other areas are given the attention of other units and/or levels.

RESEARCH

A university's activity in this area is predominantly focused on generating rigorous scientific research. To accomplish this goal, research universities support their faculty and graduate students' research agenda by providing necessary resources, advanced training, and supporting opportunities for exposure and publication in various ways such as through conferences and in-house university press houses. In addition to producing and supporting the publication of accurate, valid, and timely new knowledge, research universities educate undergraduate and graduate students in various academic disciplines and professions, with significant attention to graduate training to both support present research and create the pipeline of future researchers. Research universities tend to house multiple colleges on their main campuses, offer a wide range of academic and professional programs, offer a substantial number of graduate programs, and usually have larger class sizes, especially at the baccalaureate level.

LIBERAL EDUCATION

The central educational offer of liberal education colleges is at the undergraduate level, including baccalaureate and associate's degrees, and sometimes includes graduate programs. Liberal arts colleges' attention is on teaching undergraduate students the skills of critical thinking and providing well-rounded general education. To accomplish this task, and to provide a positive and enriching undergraduate experience, liberal arts colleges offer a wide range of programs that span the arts, humanities, and sciences, tend to have relatively small class sizes, higher faculty to student ratio, and often a strong emphasis on Greek life.

CAREER-DIRECTED EDUCATION

Career- or professions-focused institutions are chiefly aimed at educating and training undergraduate and graduate students in a variety of professions and vocations. To this end, career-focused institutions tend to offer programs that can be readily translated into employment opportunities (e.g., business administration, healthcare, education, information technology). Career-focused institutions may also offer students the opportunity to intern or otherwise associate with industry figures, thus allowing students to start building their hands-on experience and professional network while still attending school, which further supports these institutions' mission to set up their students for successful employment prospects.

It is important to emphasize that our definition of career-directed education is expressly designed to encompass a broad range of educational offerings, beyond typical vocational/technical programs. Indeed, the scoping of our project excludes many of the institutions (community colleges and technical training institutes, for example) that are major providers of vocational education. Instead, we are focused on understanding the share of institutional effort in four-year colleges and universities that is directed toward professions-oriented baccalaureate, master's degree, and certificate programs. Our assessment of Career-directed education is not normative with respect to outcomes (post-graduation employment rates, for example) but descriptive of the orientation of particular educational programs towards professions. In principle, educational programs with a Research or Liberal Education orientation are equally likely to lead to career placement and advancement; Career-directed Education programs are different only insofar as they are expressly designed to lead to employment or advancement in designated fields (e.g., finance, education, health sciences, etc.).

Enrollment profile and learning experience

Concurrent with changes in student enrollment profile, colleges and universities have been diversifying the learning experience(s) they offer. Along with a traditional learning experience that is geared toward a traditional enrollment profile, there are increasingly more opportunities for new learning experiences.

TRADITIONAL ENROLLMENT PROFILE AND FACE-TO-FACE, ON-CAMPUS, FULL-TIME LEARNING EXPERIENCE

Traditionally, young people who wished to benefit from higher education would "go away to college" to live in or near campus and immerse themselves in a living-learning environment.

This mode of provision in higher education is still highly dominant, as seen in figure 8, with 70% of all students in 2015 attending all their coursework in person, 29% attending any distance education courses, among whom 15% attend at least one, but not all of their courses online, and 14% study all of their courses online.[47]

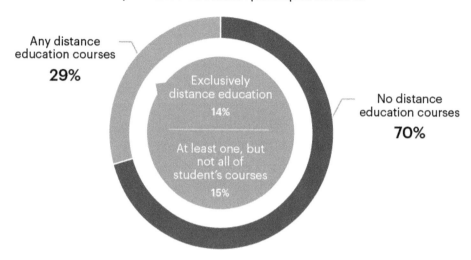

Percent of students enrolled in degree-granting postsecondary institutions

by distance education participation: 2015

Any distance education courses
29%

Exclusively distance education
14%

At least one, but not all of student's courses
15%

No distance education courses
70%

Data source: NCES, 2017.

Figure 8. Percentage of students enrolled in degree-granting postsecondary institutions, by distance education participation: 2015.

Indeed, the four-year residential education at research universities and liberal arts colleges has long been viewed by many, including educational social scientists, as the ideal expression of higher education.[48]

NEW-TRADITIONAL ENROLLMENT PROFILE AND ONLINE, OFF-CAMPUS, PART-TIME LEARNING EXPERIENCE

The presumption that college requires physical presence is no longer taken for granted in present day ideas about higher education. The technological developments of recent years have enabled institutions of higher education to develop online programs, also known as distance education, enabling students, for the first time in history, to benefit from academic schooling and attainment without ever having to set foot on campus. As shown in figure 9, about a third of students in public and nonprofit HEI take at least one, but not all of their course(s), online, while the respective percentage in for-profit HEI are about two-thirds total and as much as 86% at the graduate level.[49]

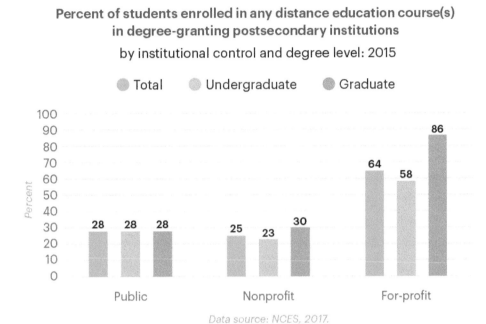

**Percent of students enrolled in any distance education course(s)
in degree-granting postsecondary institutions
by institutional control and degree level: 2015**

● Total ● Undergraduate ● Graduate

Data source: NCES, 2017.

Figure 9. Percentage of students enrolled in any distance education course(s) in degree-granting postsecondary institutions, by institutional control and degree level: 2015.

In 2015, 28% of all students in public HEI took at least one online course, with equal percentage of undergraduate and graduate students.[50] A total of 25% of students in nonprofit HEI attended at least one of their courses online, comprised of 23% of undergraduate and 30% of graduate students, and a total of 64% of all students in for-profit HEI who took at least one of their courses online, comprised of 58% undergraduate and 86% graduate students, demonstrating that for-profit HEI make far greater use of distance learning.

As reflected in figure 10, the popularity of online programs among older students, who are more likely to raise families and hold day jobs, is further demonstrated through data from 2011-2012, showing that only 3% of younger students (age 15–23) studied their entire degree online, compared to more than double (8%) of students age 24–29 and more than four times (13%) of students age 30 and older.[51]

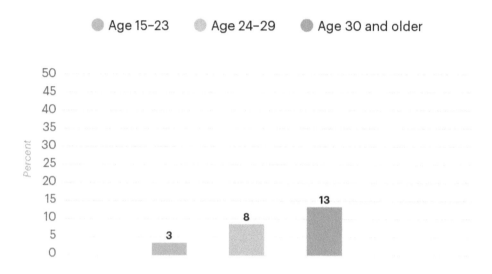

Figure 10. Percentage of students whose entire degree program is online, by age group: 2011-2012.

Part-time, night, and weekend programs enable students to participate in higher education learning, reaping the benefits of academic attainment, while not committing their full attention and time to campus life. Being able to hold a day job, care for one's family and pursue other commitments and interests is a distinctly different value proposition compared to the traditional live-on-campus one. In 2011-2012, 32.4% of undergraduate students took at least one night class and 7% took at least one weekend class.[52] As expected, students' age correlates with increased part-time attendance: in 2011-2012, 29.8% and 5.2% of younger undergraduate students (age 15–23) took at least one night or one weekend class (respectively), compared to 36.6% and 9% or older students (age 24–29), respectively.[53]

Alongside the important changes in student enrollment profiles noted here are equally notable changes in faculty demographics, including increased university reliance on "contingent" labor (non-tenured, part-time, and adjunct teaching faculty), that impact the teaching and learning environment. As the student population diversifies, there is also increasing attention to the importance of diversifying faculty ranks to address long-standing imbalances in the representation of women and people of color. The analysis presented in this report does not address the impacts of changing faculty demographics (or the related issue of university governance models) on the organization of higher education or the future of academic libraries. This is an area rich with possibility for future research.

Where do we go from here?

Major shifts in the profile of student enrollment in US higher education, and critique of the Carnegie classification, open the door to innovative ways of conceiving of US higher education institutions. A review of the literature offers new and fruitful institutional dimensions, based on which HEI can be typologized and explored. Notably, these institutional characteristics pertain to HEI's Educational Directions: Research, Liberal Education, and Career-directed Education; and to Enrollment Profile and Learning Experience: Traditional and New Traditional.

Chapter 3: Institution Typology

The US higher education system currently includes more than 4,000 postsecondary institutions, serving a broad market of students, researchers, and other economic actors (employers, research funders, and the like). To reduce the scope of the population examined in our project, the project team made a pragmatic choice to focus on nonprofit (public and private), four-year colleges, and universities.[54] Our initial project population was defined by using the 2015 Carnegie Classification to identify all nonprofit higher education institutions with a baccalaureate or higher degree program.[55]

To support our analysis of emerging library directions and the alignment of library directions with university directions, we developed a typology of prevailing institutional directions in US colleges and universities. Informed by the findings of our literature review, we concluded that this typology should include institutional characteristics beyond those captured in the commonly used Carnegie Classification, which organizes the US higher education system (primarily) according to the highest degree awarded, as well as size and level of university doctoral research activity. For our purposes, it was important to develop a model that captured institutional directions along two dimensions: educational activity (i.e., the scope of educational offerings at all degree levels) and enrollment profile. In its most comprehensive form, the Carnegie Classification includes relevant institutional attributes, such as the orientation (Arts & Sciences, Professional, etc.) of the undergraduate and graduate instructional programs. However, to address some of the important demographic characteristics that are reshaping the US higher education market (notably, the growing share of New Traditional enrollees), we felt it was necessary to include additional statistical indicators in our model.

Our approach was to combine some of the statistical indicators underpinning the Carnegie Classification with additional variable data from the national IPEDS survey of US higher education institutions.

Over a period of two months, we experimented with combining selected variables from the 2015 survey cycle for a random sample of one hundred institutions from our project population, to establish a working model of our typology. This model was refined through a process of iterative testing and validation with members of the higher education and academic library community.

By selectively extracting and cumulatively adding multiple variables, we arrived at a typology that indexes higher education institutions on two separate dimensions: (1) Educational Direction(s), and (2) Enrollment Profile and Learning Experience.

An early iteration of our typology also included a third dimension, which we tentatively labeled "religious or values-based education." It was evident from our preliminary work, in which we focused on a representative sample of 100 US colleges and universities and undertook a close examination of institutional mission statements, that many of these institutions explicitly embrace a values-centered identity. In some cases, this identity is religious (Jesuit colleges and universities, or institutions affiliated with the Southern Baptist Convention, for example), while in others it is either explicitly or implicitly secular in orientation but nonetheless directed toward particular social and cultural values (social justice, for instance). Within this dimension, we attempted to differentiate between "values-norming" institutions, where there is an explicit aim to cultivate and strengthen a core set of shared values (and sometimes to limit or even exclude competing perspectives), and "values-forming" institutions, where there is a greater emphasis on personal self-discovery and identity formation within a wide range of social norms.

Consistent with our data-driven design, we sought statistical indicators to assist in making an objective identification of institutional orientation. The Carnegie Classification, for example, includes a Community Engagement metric, based on self-assessment and validation by a national review panel.[56] However, the Carnegie Community Engagement Classification is elective, and therefore not representative of the higher education sector as a whole, nor the population subset that was the focus of our research. (It currently comprises fewer than 400 colleges and universities.) The IPEDS data set includes an indicator for institutional religious affiliation, but it too has important limitations.[57] First, and most obviously, it reflects institutional affiliation with religious sects but not mission-based pursuit of general or specific secular values (social change, for example, or the pursuit of global peace). Second, the indicator sometimes reflects a historical affiliation with a given denomination that is no longer embraced as part of the institutional mission or values. While we believe that further study of the relationship between institutional mission and the scope and purpose of academic libraries is potentially of interest, the research team concluded that it was not feasible to address in the project described here.[58]

First dimension: Educational directions

The Educational Directions dimension captures *what* institutions offer and includes three major categories. Here are the definitions, as well as our scoring formula.

- **Research** is focused on educational activity directed toward doctoral degree programs. The total Research score equals the percent of research PhD of all degrees + the percent of research expenditures (GASB or FASB) + Carnegie Classification (CC) Basic Research assigned value (IF CC=15 then 1; IF CC=16 then 0.66; IF CC=17 then 0.33).

- **Liberal Education** is focused on baccalaureate educational programming in the arts and sciences. The total Liberal Education score equals the 2015 Carnegie Classification Undergraduate (CCUG) Instructional Program Arts and Sciences assigned values (IF CCUG=6-8 then 1; IF CCUG=9-11 then 0.66; IF CCUG=12-14 then 0.5; IF CCUG=15-17 then 0.33) + percent of bachelor's of all degrees.

- **Career-directed Education** is focused on baccalaureate and master's degree programs classified as "professions-oriented," as well as non-degree certificate programs. The total Career score equals Certificates as percent of all awards (degrees + certificates) + 2015 Carnegie Classification Undergraduate (CCUG) Instructional Program Professions Plus assigned values (IF CCUG=9-11 then 0.33; IF CCUG=12-14 then 0.5; IF CCUG=15-17).

Full details on all IPEDS variables and scoring formula are included in the Institution Typology Variables and Scoring Formula table at the end of this chapter.[59]

Distribution of education directions (N=1506)

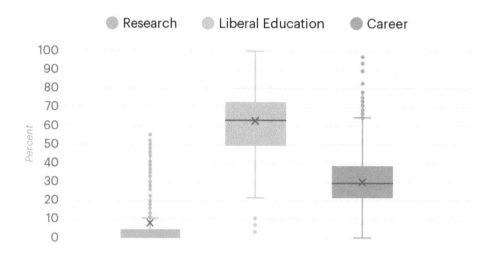

Figure 11. Distribution of Education Directions in UFLF Population (N=1506).

Figure 11 presents a series of box plots depicting the statistical distribution of institutional education directions for the project population. Box plots are conventionally used to provide a visual representation of five key statistics: the minimum and maximum thresholds of the data distribution (represented by the "T" shaped whiskers), the lower and upper quartiles (represented by the space between the whisker and the shaded box), and the middle 50 percent. Outliers are represented by dots outside the whisker. The mean is represented by an "X." Depending on the skew of the underlying data, the mean may be located above, below, or at the median (represented by a horizontal line bisecting the middle 50%).

As shown in figure 11, the mean score for Research is skewed by a number of institutional outliers where Research accounts for more than 10% of institutional educational activity. This is an important reminder that doctoral Research represents only a modest share of institutional activity in most US colleges and universities, even when community colleges are excluded from the sampling frame. By contrast, the range of scores for Liberal Education is much wider and more evenly distributed, with 50% of the population falling within the range of 50 to 72%, and a mean score near the median. While the range of Career scores is somewhat smaller (zero to 62%, with half of the population between 21 to 38%), the overall distribution is evenly spread, with about a dozen institutional outliers with exceptionally high levels of Career-directed Educational activity.

Second dimension: Enrollment profile and learning experience

The Enrollment Profile and Learning Experience dimension captures *how* institutions provide their educational offers and *for whom*. We find it useful to identify the extent to which institutions provide different learning experiences to different enrollment profiles. Each of the following, in its pure form, represents one end of the same continuum. However, almost all of the institutions in our population exhibit aspects of both:

- **Traditional Enrollment Profile, Residential Learning Experience** refers to an on-campus full-time learning experience that is primarily geared toward serving traditional student enrollment profile, i.e., full-time, on-campus learners. The total Traditional score equals the percent of full-time enrollment + the percent of students younger than age 25.

- **New-Traditional Enrollment Profile, Flexible Learning Experience** refers to an off-campus, online, part-time learning experience that is geared toward serving New Traditional student enrollment profile, e.g., part-time, distance, and adult learners and students from racial and ethnic communities and economic classes that have traditionally represented a minority share of the US higher education enterprise. The total New Traditional score equals the percent of Pell grant recipients as a share of all students + the percent of associate's degrees as a share of all degrees + the percent of part-time enrollment + the percent of "exclusively online" baccalaureate degrees + the percent of Black enrollment + the percent of Hispanic enrollment + the percent of students age 25 and older.

Most four-year institutions exhibit multiple tendencies; they have several lines of business

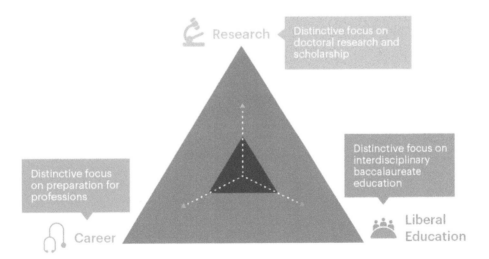

Figure 12. Institutional Education Directions.

Our institution typology accounts for the share of institutional educational activity that is dedicated to each of the three major areas of Research, Liberal Education, and Career-directed Education, and the degree to which the enrollment profile and learning experience is on the continuum between fully Traditional/Residential versus fully New Traditional/Flexible. Figure 12 illustrates the first dimension in a triangle form, with three poles representing the primary educational directions.

Using our scoring formula, we can isolate segments within the project population based on their relative position along the three educational directions. In figure 13, four segments are graphed based the institution typology scoring formula, using the mean score value for each direction. Predictably, the top scoring institutions for Research, Liberal Education and Career-directed Education exhibit very different shapes, with clear dominance of a single direction.[60] In the case of Liberal Education, the average distribution of the top 100 institutions is effectively reduced to a single dimension. The middle 50% (i.e., institutions between the 25th and 75th percentile for each direction) exhibit a prominent emphasis on Liberal Education (67%), substantial attention to Career-directed Education (33%), and negligible activity in doctoral level Research activity. The dominance of Liberal Education activity in this segment is easily explained by the continued prominence of undergraduate education as a central activity of colleges and universities in the project population. The importance of Career-directed Education in this segment provides clear evidence that institutional attention to work-ready, professions-focused education is a priority for four-year colleges and universities. This is a notable finding, given the still prevalent (though increasingly disputed) view that career education is primarily the business of community colleges and technical training institutes, rather than four-year institutions.

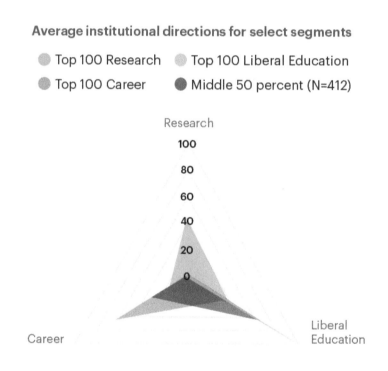

Figure 13. Average Institutional Education Directions for Select Segments.

Data Table: Average Institutional Education Directions for Select Segments (NB. Due to rounding, values presented here may not sum to 100%.)

	Average Research score	Average Liberal education score	Average Career score
Top 100 Research	45%	39%	16%
Top 100 Liberal Education	0%	99%	0%
Top 100 Career-directed Education	1%	34%	65%
Middle 50% (N=412)	1%	67%	33%

It is important to emphasize that most institutions in the project population are pursuing two or more educational directions. Indeed, as figure 13 reveals, even the top-scoring institutions in each of the three educational directions (Research, Liberal Education, and Career-directed Education) exhibits at least some institutional attention to one or more of the other areas. Of the three educational directions, Liberal Education appears to have a dominant hold on institutional identity in a plurality of institutions, most evident, of course, among the institutions in the top 100 scoring for Liberal Education. In aggregate, the average score for our population is computed to be 8% Research, 62% Liberal Education, and 30% Career-directed Education. This serves as an important reminder that the arts and sciences–based baccalaureate curriculum, and career-oriented education (at the baccalaureate and master's level, as well as non-degree certificate programs) account for more institutional activity—if not resources—than doctoral-level research.

We depict the second dimension as a continuum, represented by a bar chart measuring the relative share of Traditional/Residential and New Traditional/Flexible enrollment.

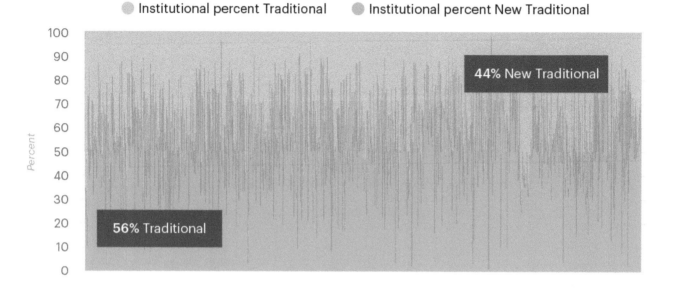

Figure 14. Traditional vs. New Traditional Enrollment Profile of University Futures, Library Futures Population (N=1506).

As shown in figure 14, almost all of the institutions in our project population support a mix of Traditional and New Traditional learners. Further analysis revealed interesting and potentially important correlations between the first and second dimensions of our model. Regression testing established a statistically significant (p<.05) correlation between the strength of an institution's score for Career-directed Education and the strength of the institution's New Traditional orientation. The institutional score for New Traditional enrollment can be predicted (with 95% confidence) from the institution's Career-directed Education score, based on this formula:

New Traditional score = 0.5709 * Career score + 0.2677, R^2 = 0.27

This finding suggests that institutions with a sizable share of New Traditional learners may have a greater need for library support related to Career-directed programming and, conversely, that institutions with a strong emphasis on Career-directed Education may need to consider whether existing library services are sufficiently adapted to the needs of New Traditional learners. By contrast, institutions with a greater Liberal Education focus are statistically more likely to have a higher average Traditional enrollment profile. The institutional score for a (historically) Traditional enrollment profile can be predicted based on this formula:

Traditional score = 0.3819 * Liberal education score + 0.3222, R^2 = 0.15

While statistically significant, the relationship between the institutional Research direction and enrollment profile was weak; the share of Traditional and New Traditional learners varies widely whether the Research score is high or low, with a slight positive correlation between the strength of the Traditional profile and Research intensity. ACRL Standards for Libraries in Higher Education emphasize the importance of establishing user-centered outcome measures for assessing library services in academic libraries of all kinds, noting that "each library must respond to its unique user population and institutional environment."[61] While every academic library will benefit from considering the demographic profile of the parent institution's enrollment profile, our findings suggest that libraries supporting a high level of Career-directed Education should be especially attentive to the service needs of New Traditional learners.

The typology presented here builds on decades of refinement and extensions to the widely used Carnegie Classification. For example, we incorporated elements of the Carnegie-defined Undergraduate Instructional Profile in our scoring formula to assist in differentiating institutions with a relatively greater emphasis on professions-oriented education, or arts and sciences–based programming.

Our typology is not intended as a replacement to the Carnegie Classification, but rather as an elaboration of it, specifically designed to highlight the diversity of US higher education with respect to educational directions and changing student demographics. A key benefit of our approach is that it enables researchers (and, we hope, academic and library administrators) to detect converging, or diverging, institutional directions within and across the basic Carnegie categories. Thus, within our typology, one can identify institutional cohorts that share a strong Career-directed Education focus at the baccalaureate, master's, or doctoral level; or isolate a subset of institutions with a similar enrollment profile and educational focus, without regard to highest-degree awarded (the primary analytical unit of the basic Carnegie Classification). From a strategic planning perspective—within and beyond the library—we believe the typology has particular value precisely because it avoids framing the higher education enterprise in terms of the highest level of degree conferred by a given institution.

To illustrate the utility of our typology, it is helpful to consider how the basic Carnegie Classification obscures some important differences in institutional identity. For instance, within the broad category of Doctoral universities, the range of Research activity computed by our scoring formula is 0.40 (Minimum=0.15, Maximum=0.55).[62] The range of Research scores for Master's institutions is 0.27 (Minimum=0.00, Maximum=0.27). The range of Research scores for Baccalaureate institutions is 0.14 (Minimum=0.00, Maximum=0.14). These data suggest that some Master's institutions in the Carnegie basic classification have a stronger Research direction than institutions' in the Doctoral universities category. And, while no Baccalaureate institution achieves the minimum threshold of Research in Doctoral universities, the most Research-directed institutions in the Carnegie basic Baccalaureate category score very close (0.14 versus 0.15).[63] From a library planning/assessment perspective, it may be more reasonable for institutions to benchmark service quality based on peer groups derived from our educational direction scores, rather than basic Carnegie categories.

The tables below summarize the range of educational direction scores for each of the broad institutional categories in the Carnegie Classification represented in our project population of 1,506 institutions.[64] As can be seen, Baccalaureate, Master's, and Doctoral institutions exhibit distinctive profiles in our three educational directions. As noted, Doctoral institutions have the highest average score for Research; Baccalaureate institutions score highest for Liberal Education; Master's institutions score highest for Career-directed Education. What is more significant, however, is the variability in educational directions for each of these broad Carnegie categories. Thus, our typology reveals a more nuanced picture of the range of institutional identities within general categories of degree-granting colleges and universities, as well as across those categories.

Data Tables: Educational Direction Scores Represented by Project Population Summarized (N=1,506).

Research	Baccalaureate institutions (N=515)	Master's instituions (N=680)	Doctoral institutions (N=310)
Mean	0.01	0.01	0.33
Median	0.00	0.00	0.34
Range	0.14	0.27	0.40
Minimum	0.00	0.00	0.15
Maximum	0.14	0.27	0.55

Liberal education	Baccalaureate institutions (N=515)	Master's instituions (N=680)	Doctoral institutions (N=310)
Mean	0.74	0.62	0.44
Median	0.74	0.63	0.43
Range	0.88	0.97	0.65
Minimum	0.12	0.03	0.12
Maximum	1.00	1.00	0.77

Career-directed education	Baccalaureate institutions (N=515)	Master's instituions (N=680)	Doctoral institutions (N=310)
Mean	0.26	0.37	0.23
Median	0.26	0.37	0.23
Range	0.83	0.97	0.59
Minimum	0.00	0.00	0.00
Maximum	0.83	0.97	0.26

A note on the evolution of institutional directions

Our institution typology is based on analysis of data from the 2015 IPEDS institutional survey cycle. As such, it represents a fixed point in time, and an intrinsic limitation in our research design. It was not feasible, within the constraints of this project, to identify a core set of variable data for which a time series could be analyzed. This is due, in part, to ongoing evaluation and improvements in the IPEDS institutional survey (new variables are introduced over time; other variables are superseded or eliminated) but also the limitations of longitudinal surveys in which participation varies year over year.

The research team attempted to compile a ten-year longitudinal data set to examine changes in educational direction and enrollment profile, but it was soon established that certain variables important to our study (the number of fully online baccalaureate degrees, for example, or the undergraduate instructional profile) were not available for the desired time horizon, and that the already modest population size would need to be further reduced to ensure that reporting was available for each year. In the end, we concluded that it was preferable to use the most comprehensive and current data available for a larger number of institutions, rather than developing a scoring formula that depended on a smaller set of variables.

Anecdotally, we can report that our review of longitudinal data did suggest some movement in institutional educational direction over time as well as (more predictably) changes in the enrollment profile, with a growing share of New Traditional students in most institutions. Broadly speaking, the data suggested that at least some institutions with an historical emphasis on Liberal Education were broadening their educational offer to move in the direction of Career-directed Education, and some Research-oriented institutions were likewise diversifying their offerings to include more professional master's and certificate programs.[65] This represents a potentially interesting area for further research, with important implications for strategic planning in academic libraries.

	Research	Liberal Education	Career	Traditional	New Traditional
Primary variables (IPEDS institutional characteristics)	Doctor's degree - research/scholarship (DRVC2015)	Carnegie Classification 2015: Undergraduate Instructional Program (HD2015)	Carnegie Classification 2015: Undergraduate Instructional Program (HD2015)	Full-time enrollment (DRVEF2015)	Percent of undergraduate students awarded Pell grants (SFA1415)
	Doctor's degree - professional practice (DRVC2015)	Bachelor's degree (DRVC2015)	Certificates of 2 but less than 4-years (DRVC2015)	Total enrollment (DRVEF2015)	12-month full-time equivalent enrollment: 2014-15 (DRVEF122015)
	Doctor's degree - other (DRVC2015)	Doctor's degree - research/scholarship (DRVC2015)	Certificates of 1 but less than 2-years (DRVC2015)	Grand total (EF2015B All students total age under 25 total)	Number of students receiving an associate's degree (DRVC2015)
	Research expenses as a percent of total core expenses (GASB) (DRVF2015)	Doctor's degree - professional practice (DRVC2015)	Certificates of less than 1-year (DRVC2015)	Grand total (EF2015A All students total)	Part-time enrollment (DRVEF2015)
	Research expenses as a percent of total core expenses (FASB) (DRVF2015)	Doctor's degree - other (DRVC2015)	Postbaccalaureate certificates (DRVC2015)		Percent of students enrolled exclusively in distance education courses (DRVEF2015)
	Carnegie Classification 2015: Basic (HD2015)	Master's degree (DRVC2015)	Post-master's certificates (DRVC2015)		Black or African American total (EF2015A All students total)
		Associate's degree (DRVC2015)	Doctor's degree - research/scholarship (DRVC2015)		Hispanic total (EF2015A All students total)
			Doctor's degree - professional practice (DRVC2015)		Grand total (EF2015B All students total age 25 and over total)
			Doctor's degree - other (DRVC2015)		
			Master's degree (DRVC2015)		
			Bachelor's degree (DRVC2015)		
			Associate's degree (DRVC2015)		
Derived variables	Research doctorate as percent of all degrees	Bachelors as percent of all degrees	Certificates as percent of all awards (degrees + certificates)	Percent students under age 25	Derived grand total students 25 and over
	GASB or FASB research expenses as a percent of total core expenses (DRVF2015)	Liberal arts score: 2015 Carnegie Classification Undergraduate Instructional Program Art and Sciences assigned values: IF CCUG=6-8 then1; IF CCUG=9-11 then 0.66; IF CCUG=12-14 then 0.5; IF CCUG=15-17 then 0.33	Carnegie Classification Undergraduate Instructional Program Professions Plus assigned values: IF CCUG=9-11 then 0.33; IF CCUG=12-14 then 0.5; IF CCUG=15-17 then 0.66; IF CCUG=18-20 then 1	Full-time enrollment as percent of total enrollment	Percent students age 25 and over
	CC Basic Research assigned values: IF CC=15 then 1; IF CC=16 then 0.66; IF CC=17 then 0.33				Derived percent Black students
					Derived percent Hispanic students
					Part-time enrollment as percent of total enrollment
Total scoring formula	Total Research score = % research PhD of all degrees + % research expenditures (GASB or FASB) + Carnegie Classification Basic Research assigned value	Total Liberal Education score = Carnegie Classification Undergraduate Instructional Program Arts and Sciences assigned values + % of bachelors of all degrees	Total Career score = Certificates as percent of all awards (degrees + certificates) + Carnegie Classification Undergraduate Instructional Program Professions Plus assigned values	Total Residential score = % full-time enrollment + % of students under age 25	Total Convenience score = % Pell grantees of all students + % associates degrees of all degrees + % part-time enrollment + % exclusively distance learning + % Black enrollment + % Hispanic enrollment + % students age 25 and over

Figure 15. Institutional Typology Variables and Scoring Formula..

Chapter 4: Library Services Framework

For purposes of this project, we defined library services as *the outputs that libraries produce in order to serve their constituencies*. With a research population of public and private nonprofit academic institutions in the US that grant a bachelor's degree or higher, we designed this framework to be broadly inclusive. Specifically, it must be meaningful at institutions with both research and instructional emphases in their mission, as well as residential, commuter, and distance models for instructional delivery and student experience.

To develop this framework, we started from the bottom up. We reviewed the websites and planning documents from dozens of academic libraries selected at random from across the higher education landscape. The individual library services they offer vary across institution types, and they have nomenclature that can sometimes vary as well. We came up with dozens of individual services. We continued reviewing individual institutions until we no longer saw new services emerging from this review process.

This approach was not designed, however, to capture every single service offering. Rather, we were gathering individual services in order to design a framework of key services areas. We knew from the project's inception that we could not possibly hope to gather data on dozens of discrete services. Instead, by grouping them into key services areas, we hoped to find a signal about institutional type difference rather than get caught up in the noisy environment of individual services that differ at an institutional level. We reviewed a draft of the key services areas with a variety of library leaders, and we revised the framework accordingly.

Because we defined services as outputs, it was notable in our testing of the draft services framework that it can be difficult for leaders to distinguish the library's resources from its outputs. To ensure that readers make this distinction clearly, here are some of the library's resources, or assets, or inputs, which are not services:

- Employees and their expertise
- Materials budget, endowments, and other monetary resources
- The on- and off-campus spaces that the library owns, occupies, or controls
- Collections that the library owns, licenses, or otherwise can rely upon
- Collaborative agreements, standards, and platforms that allow it to collaborate with other libraries

Library space presents an interesting case. While physical space, in and of itself, is not a service, it can be strategically deployed to support a range of library services. Given that some of our reviewers felt strongly the absence of a specific call-out around space as a service in our framework, we added "Provide Study Space" as a service area.

Academic libraries have been rethinking their strategic directions and services portfolios. The services framework we eventually arrived at includes the following nine key areas:

- Convene Campus Community: Provide spaces and facilitate programs for the community broadly or specific sub-populations to generate engagement, outreach, and inclusion.

- Enable Academic Success[66]: Support instruction, facilitate learning, improve information literacy, and/or maximize retention, progression, graduation, and later life success.

- Facilitate Information Access: Enable discovery and usage of information resources of any format or ownership; provide for preservation of general collections.

- Foster Scholarship and Creation: Deliver expertise, assistance, tools, and services that support research and creative work.

- Include and Support Off-Campus Users: Provide equitable access for part-time students, distance and online learners, and other principally off-campus/non-campus/remote users.

- Preserve and Promote Unique Collections: Ensure the long-term stewardship of rare materials and special collections, and maximize their usage.

- Provide Study Space: Provide physical spaces for academic collaboration, quiet study, and technology-enhanced instruction and/or learning.

- Showcase Scholarly Expertise: Promote research excellence and subject matter expertise of scholars and other affiliates; includes repository activities for open access preprint materials.

- Transform Scholarly Publishing: Drive toward modernized formats, revamped business models, and reduced market concentration.

While necessarily imperfect, this framework provides us with a way of measuring academic library alignment across many institution types. We hope that this framework provides academic libraries with a mechanism for thinking about their services areas that can allow them to be more systematic in their own planning, as a side benefit of the project.

Chapter 5. Key Findings and Implications

Survey methodology

A survey questionnaire was developed for library directors to address how they perceived their institution to fit into the typology we had developed and how they allocated resources, and expected to do so, relative to the key services areas. After being drafted and refined by the project team, the survey instrument was tested in a series of cognitive interviews with members of our survey population.

Our survey sample was carefully prepared to target the 1,506 institutions profiled in our typology plus others that would have been included in our typology had they not been missing IPEDS data. We excluded the several cases where a library was known to us to provide services on a shared basis to multiple higher education institutions. For every other institution, we attempted to collect name and email address for the directors of the principal campus library (i.e., not the medical, law, or other library if it is part of a separate reporting line). In a small number of cases, it was impossible to locate contact information. We sent invitation messages to 1,477 individuals.

Invitation messages were sent to all sample members on November 20, 2017. The sample was randomly divided such that half of the invitations were sent under the signature of Lorcan Dempsey and half under the signature of Deanna Marcum. On November 28, 2017, a reminder message was generated to non-respondents such that each was signed by the other individual from the first message. A second reminder to non-respondents was generated on January 16, 2018, this time under the signature of Constance Malpas or Roger Schonfeld. Based on response rate, no further reminders were sent.

The survey was closed on February 5, 2018. A total of 581 responses were incorporated into the final dataset. A small number of responses (26) were received from institutions not included in our typology. Our final response rate was 39.3%. Response rates for individual questions may vary due to skip patterns and non-response.

To ensure that analysis of all survey data uses the same dataset, in all analysis that follows, we exclude the 26 responses that came from institutions not included in our typology. Analysis is further limited to institutions that provided complete responses to relevant questions.

Survey findings: university and library directions

In this section, we offer several outlooks on the survey data regarding university educational directions and library directions. We begin with key descriptive statistics and then provide two analytical perspectives on the data.

DESCRIPTIVE STATISTICS

We first examined directional differences along the three axes of educational activity in our model, based on percentile distributions. For Research activity, the average difference between institutional emphasis and library emphasis is -3 points, indicating that overall respondents consider the institutional emphasis on Research to be slightly less than library attention and support for this area. The middle 50% of respondents reported a difference between 0 and -5 points for institutional Research emphasis compared to library emphasis. In other words, half of respondents reported the difference between institutional emphasis and library emphasis fell between zero (no difference in direction) and -5 points (the institutional emphasis on research is slightly less than the library emphasis). The other half of respondents reported a difference between -5 and -100 points (lower 25%) or between zero and 46 (upper 25%). Despite high variation at the extremes, the overall variance is modest.

The average difference between institutional and library attention to Liberal Education is -4 points, again suggesting a modest gap with the library investing slightly more attention to this area than the university as a whole. The middle 50% of respondents report a difference of between zero and -10 points in institutional activity and library activity supporting Liberal Education. The bottom 25% of respondents report a difference between -10 and -50 points in institutional and library directions; the upper 25% report a difference between zero and 80 points.

The greatest difference between institutional directions and library directions relates to Career-directed Education, with an average difference of 7 points. On average, respondents report that the parent institution is more focused on Career-directed Educational activity than the library is. The upper 25 percent reported a difference between 10 and 50 points. The middle 50 percent of respondents reported a difference between zero and 10 points. The lower 25 percent of respondents reported a difference between zero and -60 points in institutional and library activity supporting Career-directed Education. Thus, the overall finding is that

library directors in our survey perceive that the parent institution places a greater emphasis on work-ready educational programs than is reflected in current library activity.

As these results suggest, perceptions regarding the fit of local library services and institutional educational priorities vary widely. The upper and lower bounds of variation are high and, for a handful of extreme outliers, library and institutional directions reportedly diverge widely. At the opposite end of the spectrum, nearly a quarter of respondents report that library priorities are in perfect alignment with perceived institutional priorities. Between these poles, a substantial share of library directors report a gap between library activity and the perceived educational priorities of the institution the library serves. This finding is consistent with the results of our typological analysis of institutions within the University Futures, Library Futures sample frame. As noted in Chapter Three, IPEDS survey data indicate that the educational directions of the 1,506 colleges and universities in our project population differ significantly, from colleges with a "100%" focus on liberal education to universities that are expanding career-ready educational programming, and rebalancing investments in doctoral research and the undergraduate arts and sciences curriculum. It is reasonable to suppose that expectations of library services, and the current fit of library services to institutional priorities, will differ in these settings.

We first compared respondent perceptions of educational directions at their institutions to the directions revealed by our analysis of IPEDS data for the same institutions.[67] The purpose of this was twofold: first, to establish how library directors perceive their institutions to be "spread" across

Research, Liberal Education, and Career-directed Educational activity; and, second, to evaluate the extent to which their views diverge from or converge with directions reflected in our institution typology.

Only modest differences are observable in the average values: library directors reported an average 14% Research, 47% Liberal Education, and 39% Career-directed Education for perceived institutional directions. (Standard deviations: .15, .23, and .22 respectively.) The corresponding average values from our analysis of IPEDS values for these institutions are 10% Research, 63% Liberal Education, and 28% Career-directed Education.[68] (Standard deviations:.14, .18, .16) Figure 16 provides a visual representation of institutional directions reported by survey respondents, compared to institutional directions as they are modeled in our typology.

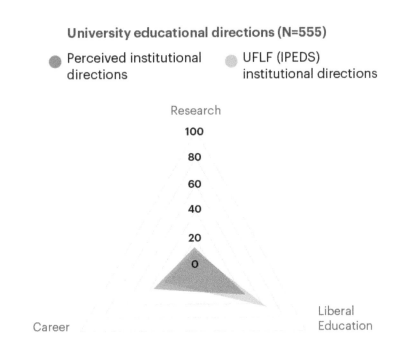

Figure 16. University Educational Directions (N=555).

Data table: University Educational Directions (N=555)

	Research	Liberal education	Career
Perceived institutional directions	14%	47%	39%
UFLF IPEDS institutional directions	10%	63%	28%

The difference between perceived and IPEDS-based educational directions is greatest in the area of Liberal education. Respondents perceived institutional activity in Liberal Education to be 15 points lower than institutional directions in our typology. Library directors appear to feel that Career-directed Education is a slightly greater share of institutional activity (+11 points) than is captured by our institution typology. This may reflect a growing concern that colleges and universities need to more effectively demonstrate that they are delivering workforce-relevant education. While our survey explicitly defined Career-directed Education as "Baccalaureate, master's, and non-degree certificate programs in specific professional fields (e.g., business management, criminal justice, education, health care)," some respondents may have applied a broader definition, resulting in a higher assessment of related institutional activity.

Comparing perceived institutional directions to perceived library directions for this same population, it is apparent that library directors generally feel there is a good fit between library support and institutional educational directions. This is perhaps not a particularly surprising finding, as survey respondents might be reluctant to report a substantial directional difference between library operations and university educational activity. The average reported library directions are: 17% Research, 51% Liberal Education, and 32% Career. (Standard deviations: .18, .23 and .20, respectively.)

Figure 17. University Directions vs. Library Directions (N=555).

Data table: University Directions vs Library Directions (N=555)

	Research	Liberal education	Career
Perceived institutional directions	14%	47%	39%
Perceived library directions	17%	51%	32%

A more nuanced view of library directors' perceptions of the "fit" of library activity and institutional activity is revealed when we examine the relative distribution of responses. Almost a quarter of respondents (23%) reported that library directions map perfectly to institutional directions; i.e., there is no reported difference in library or institutional emphasis on any educational direction.

A small fraction of respondents (2%) reported a difference of 50 points or more along any of the educational directions. One extreme outlier reported a 100 point difference between institutional emphasis on research (zero emphasis), and library activity supporting this activity (100% emphasis). Overall, as reflected in figure 17, the reported differences in institutional and library directions were very small.

ANALYTICAL PERSPECTIVES

The first analytical perspective relies on existing affinity groups (ARL, Oberlin, UIA); the second analytical perspective utilizes our institution typology to identify groups of institutions with similar educational directions. To support this second approach, we segmented our survey responses into five categories. The first three categories comprise the top 100 institutions in each of the primary educational directions (Research, Liberal Education, and Career). A fourth category comprises institutions that fall within the 25th and 75th percentile of the distribution for each of these directions; i.e., institutions in the middle range of Research and Liberal Education and Career. A fifth category comprises 100 institutions with the highest New Traditional Enrollment Profile and Learning Experience score.[69]

To explore the extent to which perceptions of library direction vary in different segments of the higher education community (within the limits of our study population), we performed a segmented analysis of survey responses in a few well-known affinity groups: members of the Association of Research Libraries, Oberlin Group libraries, and members of the University Innovation Alliance. (Despite our best efforts and extensive community consultation, the research team was not able to identify an existing affinity group that could be used as a proxy for Career-directed eEucation institutions. It was not feasible, for example, to segment the project population into members of continuing education and professional education organizations such as UCPEA or AACE.[70]) The survey response rate for each of these groups exceeded 33% in each case. Below, we compare the responses of each group to the directions reflected in our institution typology and then examine differences between the perceived directions of library emphasis and institutional emphasis.

ARL directors perceive institutional educational directions to be somewhat more evenly distributed across Research, Liberal Education and Career-directed Education than is reflected in our institution typology. The greatest disparity relates to Career-directed Education, with respondents indicating an average 11-point difference between self-reported institutional activity and scoring based on IPEDS data. While respondents perceive institutional Research activity to be greater than other categories, similar to what is reflected in our typology, they report lower Research and Educational activity overall. By contrast, perceptions of university attention to Career-directed Education are greater than our model suggests.

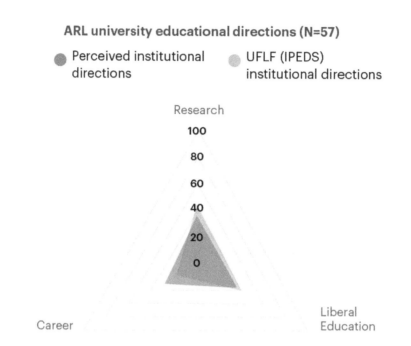

ARL university educational directions (N=57)

● Perceived institutional directions   ● UFLF (IPEDS) institutional directions

Figure 18. ARL University Educational Directions (N=57).

Data table: ARL University Educational Directions (N=57)

	Research	Liberal education	Career
Perceived institutional directions	38%	34%	28%
UFLF (IPEDS) institutional directions	44%	40%	17%

With respect to the perceived alignment of library directions and institutional directions, ARL directors reported a remarkably close fit. Directors reported a near perfect alignment with institutional Research directions, and a 5-point difference for Liberal Education, with the library pulling out slightly ahead of the overall institutional directions. Conversely, in the area of Career-directed Education, respondents reported that the institution had a modestly greater (+5 points) emphasis than the library. This suggests that ARL directors recognize that universities prioritize career-related programming somewhat more than is reflected in library services investments.

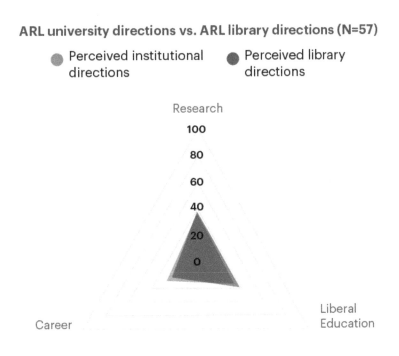

ARL university directions vs. ARL library directions (N=57)

● Perceived institutional directions   ● Perceived library directions

Research

100
80
60
40
20
0

Career   Liberal Education

Figure 19. ARL University Directions vs. ARL Library Directions (N=57).

Data table: ARL University Directions vs. ARL Library Directions (N=57)

	Research	Liberal education	Career
Perceived institutional directions	38%	34%	28%
Perceived library directions	39%	39%	23%

Like ARL directors, Oberlin Group respondents perceive Career-directed Education to be a greater institutional focus than is reflected in our analysis of IPEDS data. However, there is agreement that Liberal Education is by far the dominant institutional focus, exceeding 80% of educational activity. The 2-point gap in Research activity, which Oberlin Group library directors perceive as higher (3%) than is reflected in our institution typology (1%) may be attributed to an emphasis on undergraduate research, generally viewed as a hallmark of excellence in institutions emphasizing liberal education. Scoring in our institution typology is based on doctoral level research activity, rather than undergraduate research.

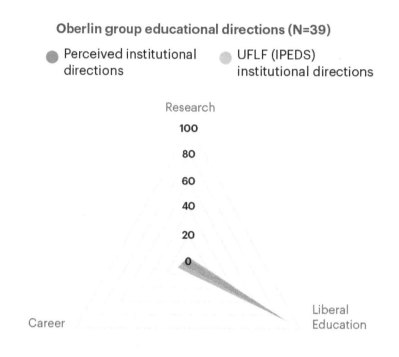

Oberlin group educational directions (N=39)

● Perceived institutional directions ○ UFLF (IPEDS) institutional directions

Figure 20. Oberlin Group Educational Directions (N=39).

Data table: Oberlin Group Educational Directions (N=39)

	Research	Liberal education	Career
Perceived institutional directions	3%	86%	11%
UFLF (IPEDS) institutional directions	1%	93%	6%

When asked to evaluate library support for different areas of educational activity, Oberlin Group respondents, like ARL directors, reported very close alignment. In keeping with perceived institutional priorities, library support was almost entirely directed toward support of the undergraduate Liberal Education curriculum, with a modest margin of +3 points in library emphasis.

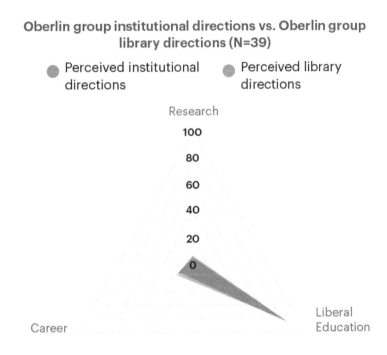

Oberlin group institutional directions vs. Oberlin group library directions (N=39)

● Perceived institutional directions   ● Perceived library directions

Figure 21. Oberlin Group Institutional Directions vs. Library Directions (N=39).

Data table: Oberlin Group Institutional Directions vs. Library Directions (N=39)

	Research	Liberal education	Career
Perceived institutional directions	2%	83%	15%
Perceived library directions	3%	86%	11%

Thus, Oberlin Group library directors perceive virtually no difference between their parent institutions' directions versus library directions. Interestingly, though, they do perceive a shortfall in library support for Career-directed programs, even in institutions where professions-focused degree production is relatively low. This finding mirrors the parallel finding for ARL library directors.

The third and last affinity group we analyzed is the University Innovation Alliance (UIA), a coalition of public research universities "committed to increasing the number and diversity of college graduates in the United States."[71] This group is of particular interest for our project, because it represents a cohort of institutions that are moving in a common direction, with deliberate purpose. They are examining and revising institutional educational directions to the base of participation in higher education and improve student outcomes. As such, they represent an interesting natural experiment for our project: is clarity of purpose in university educational directions mirrored in library directions? Notwithstanding the small size of this group (and correspondingly small N for our analysis), we include here as a potentially instructive example.

UIA university educational directions (N=7)

● Perceived institutional directions ● UFLF (IPEDS) institutional directions

Research
100
80
60
40
20
0

Career

Liberal Education

Figure 22. UIA University Educational Directions (N=7).

Data table: UIA University Educational Directions (N=7)

	Research	Liberal education	Career
Perceived institutional directions	33%	31%	36%
UFLF (IPEDS) institutional directions	42%	39%	19%

UIA survey respondents' perceptions of institutional direction are largely consistent with what is reflected in our institution typology. Library directors report that Research represents a somewhat smaller share of institutional activity than is reflected in IPEDS, but overall there is agreement that Research and Liberal Education claim an equal share of institutional attention. However, our institution typology suggests that UIA institutional directions have a smaller relative share of institutional activity in Career-directed education than is reflected in survey responses. As noted in our discussion of focus group interview findings (below), library directors from UIA institutions affirmed that increased institutional attention to improving student success (including outcome measurements such as job placement rates of recent graduates) has stimulated increased awareness of Career-directed Education within the library, and a growing conviction that the library should have a role in preparing students for "post-graduation" success.

UIA institutional directions vs. UIA library directions (N=7)

Figure 23. UIA Institutional Directions vs. Library Directions (N=7).

Data table: UIA Institutional Directions vs. Library Directions (N=7)

	Research	Liberal education	Career
Perceived institutional directions	33%	31%	36%
UFLF (IPEDS) institutional directions	42%	39%	19%

Interestingly, UIA survey respondents acknowledge a gap of 10 points between library vs. institutional attention to Career-directed Education. Again, this suggests that library directors in this group are attentive to the apparent divergence of library directions from larger institutional directions in an area (e.g., workforce readiness) that is of growing importance in US higher education generally, and directly pertinent to the UIA's ambition to transform the university enterprise. It remains to be seen if UIA libraries will move more assertively to close this gap than other academic research libraries.

ANALYTICAL PERSPECTIVES DERIVED FROM INSTITUTION TYPOLOGY

Now we turn to the second analytical perspective on institutional and library directions, based on groupings derived from our institution typology.

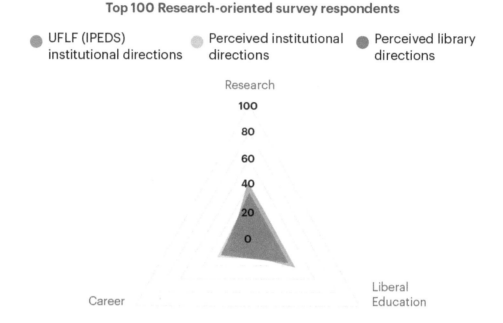

Top 100 Research-oriented survey respondents

● UFLF (IPEDS)
institutional directions

○ Perceived institutional
directions

● Perceived library
directions

Research

100

80

60

40

20

0

Career   Liberal
Education

Figure 24. Top 100 Research-oriented Survey Respondent Institutional Directions (N=100).

Data table: Top 100 Research-oriented survey respondent institutional directions (N=100)

	Research	Liberal education	Career
UFLF (IPEDS) institutional directions	41%	41%	19%
Perceived institutional directions	35%	35%	31%
Perceived library directions	36%	38%	26%

Survey respondents from the top 100 Research-oriented institutions perceive institutional and library directions to be more evenly distributed across the three directions than is reflected in our institution typology. Specifically, they report a stronger directional emphasis on Career-directed Education. They report the university library directions to be highly congruent with these perceived educational directions.

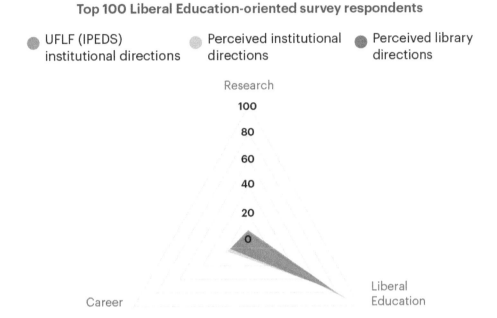

Top 100 Liberal Education-oriented survey respondents

- UFLF (IPEDS) institutional directions
- Perceived institutional directions
- Perceived library directions

Figure 25. Top 100 Liberal education-oriented survey respondent institutional directions (N=100).

Data table: Top 100 Liberal education-oriented survey respondent institutional directions (N=100)

	Research	Liberal education	Career
UFLF (IPEDS) institutional directions	41%	41%	19%
Perceived institutional directions	35%	35%	31%
Perceived library directions	36%	38%	26%

Comparing responses of library directors from the top 100 Liberal Education institutions among our survey respondents, it is apparent that their perceptions of Career emphasis are greater than revealed by our institution typology, which, in fact, rates the average Liberal Education character somewhat higher.

Top 100 Career-oriented survey respondents

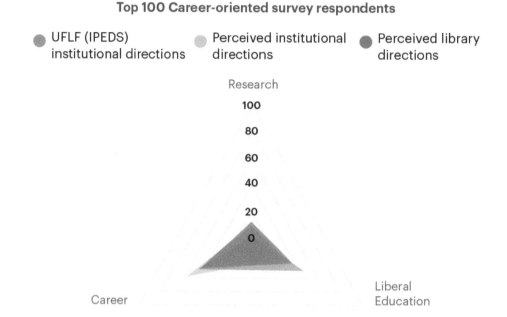

Figure 26. Top 100 Career-oriented survey respondent institutional directions (N=100).

Data table: Top 100 Career-oriented survey respondent institutional directions (N=100)

	Research	Liberal education	Career
UFLF (IPEDS) institutional directions	1%	50%	48%
Perceived institutional directions	11%	33%	57%
Perceived library directions	16%	37%	47%

Among the 100 survey respondents with the highest Career emphasis, there is a shared perception that Career-related Education and Research activities are more dominant than Liberal Education. This contrasts somewhat with the directions revealed by the institution typology, which suggests a more even distribution of educational activity in Liberal Education and Career-directed Education, and less Research activity.

Top 100 New Traditional-oriented survey respondents

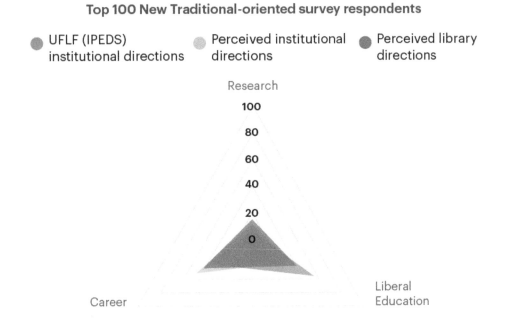

Figure 27. Top 100 New Traditional-oriented Survey Respondents.

Data table: Top 100 New Traditional-oriented Survey Respondents (N=100)

	Research	Liberal education	Career
UFLF (IPEDS) institutional directions	6	56	38
Perceived institutional directions	13	36	51
Perceived library directions	17	40	43

Among the top 100 New Traditional-oriented survey respondents, directors reported a greater Research and Career orientation and a lesser Liberal Education orientation than is reflected in our institution typology. This is true both for institutional directions and library directions.

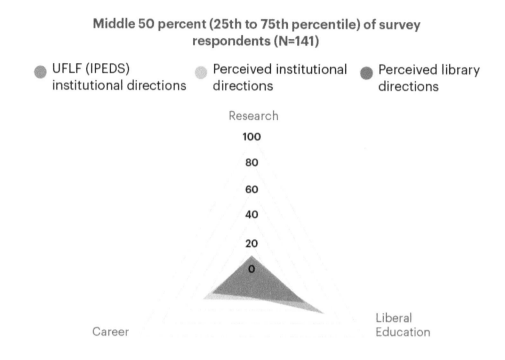

Middle 50 percent (25th to 75th percentile) of survey respondents (N=141)

● UFLF (IPEDS) institutional directions   ● Perceived institutional directions   ● Perceived library directions

Figure 28. Middle 50%(25th to 75th percentile) of Survey Respondents (N=141).

Data table: Middle 50% (25th to 75th percentile) for Research, Liberal education, and Career (N=141)

	Research	Liberal education	Career
UFLF (IPEDS) institutional directions	2	67	31
Perceived institutional directions	10	46	44
Perceived library directions	13	50	37

Looking at survey respondents situated between the 25th and 75th percentile distribution for Research, Liberal Education and Career-directed activity, it emerges that library directors perceive institutional directions to be almost evenly distributed across these three areas. This contrasts with the "middle" distribution in the typology, which is characterized by a slightly greater emphasis on Liberal education. This is consistent with the population parameters described in Chapter Three. Library directors in this segment also perceive library emphases to be evenly distributed.

To summarize, the key findings from our analysis of institution and library directions, as measured by our institution typology and reported by survey respondents:

- **Library director perceptions of institutional educational directions are similar to directions represented in the institutional typology.** ARL directors perceive a greater institutional Research emphasis than directors in Oberlin Group institutions (who perceived a greater Liberal Education emphasis). They are clearly aware of the primary educational direction of their institutions.

- Overall, **directors believe current library directions are closely aligned with institutional directions.**

- Respondents report **library attention to Research and Liberal Education is slightly greater than institutional activity in these areas.** By contrast, they acknowledge a gap between institutional attention to Career-directed Education and library support for this activity

- Comparing typology-based segmentation to existing affinity groups, we find that our institution typology reliably characterizes known institution types with the significant added advantage that **the typology can be used to test institutional directions for colleges and universities not formally affiliated with affinity groups** such as ARL, Oberlin Group, etc. This is potentially important in identifying relevant peer groups for benchmarking or collaborative partnerships.

UNIVERSITY AND LIBRARY SUPPORT FOR TRADITIONAL AND NEW TRADITIONAL STUDENTS

Survey respondents were asked to evaluate the balance of educational programming for Traditional (residential and full-time) students and New Traditional students (adult and part-time students, as well as traditionally underserved populations). Respondents were instructed to make a "best guess" based on individual perceptions of the institution, rather than seeking out detailed enrollment data or information about the full range of pedagogical approaches in use.

Of the survey respondents included in our institution typology, a total of 489 (88%) provided a rating of institutional and library support for what we termed "Residential v. Flexible/Convenience" educational models. For ease of reference, but also to highlight the relationship between the changing demographics of higher education and adoption of more inclusive pedagogies, we characterize flexible/convenience educational models as those designed to accommodate New Traditional students—acknowledging that full-time, residential students may benefit as much from access to online courses and the like as do part-time, first-generation, or adult learners.[72]

As shown in Figure 29, survey respondents generally perceived institutional support for New Traditional students to be less than is measured in our typology, for these same 489 institutions. Our IPEDS-based scoring reflects an average 39% emphasis on New Traditional learners, compared to a 28% emphasis reported by survey respondents. We do not regard the size of this gap to be especially significant, as library directors do not necessarily have direct knowledge of the college or university enrollment profile, and opinions about what constitutes an institutional accommodation for different learners will vary. Nevertheless, it is noteworthy that respondents generally viewed the dominant institutional profile to be more Traditional (residential, full-time) than not.

Percent of institutional attention to New Traditional students: Institution typology vs. survey (N=489)

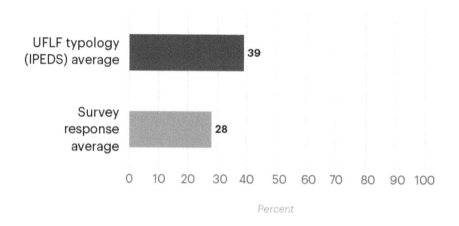

Figure 29. Share of Institutional Attention to New Traditional Students: Institution Typology vs. Survey (N=489).

Respondents were further asked to report on the balance of library support for Traditional and New Traditional students, and related educational programming. The intent of this question was to elicit feedback on perceptions of library activity and attention, as opposed to an inventory of services. Figure 30 compares respondent perceptions of library support and institutional attention to these learners, revealing that library directors generally view the library having a greater emphasis on flexibility and accommodation. This may reflect the growing emphasis on user-centered design and attention to user experience in all facets of library service provision, from attention to compliance with accessibility standards in physical and online environments to implementing equity, diversity, and inclusion policies that reaffirm the library's central mission of providing access for all.

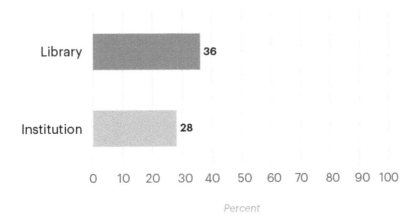

Percent of library vs. institutional attention to New Traditional students (N=489 respondents)

Figure 30. Survey Respondents' Perceptions of Institutional vs. Library Attention to New Traditional Students (N=489).

A segmented analysis of respondent perceptions based on affinity groups reveals a similar pattern with respect to library support of New Traditional learners. Library directors from ARL, Oberlin Group, and UIA institutions all reported that library support for part-time, online and other flexible modes of educational participation are greater than the overall direction of the institution. UIA respondents reported the smallest proportional gap between institutional and library support, while Oberlin group respondents reported the largest gap. Oberlin group respondents also perceived institutional support for New Traditional learners to be substantially lower than was reported by other groups.

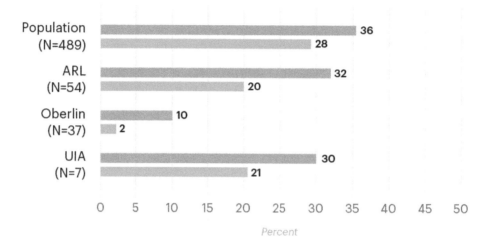

Percent of perceived attention to New Traditional students: population and selected segments

● Perceived library support for New Traditional students

● Perceived institutional support for New Traditional students

Figure 31. Perceptions of Institutional and Library Attention to New Traditional Students; Population and Selected Segments.

ANALYTICAL PERSPECTIVES DERIVED FROM INSTITUTION TYPOLOGY

Here, we repeat the approach to segmented analysis based on our institution typology, focused on survey respondents with the top 100 scores in Research, Liberal Education, and Career-directed Education, as well as institutions with a score between the 25th and 75th percentile for these directions.

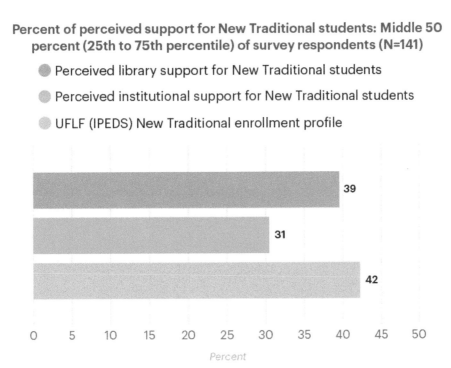

Percent of perceived support for New Traditional students: Middle 50 percent (25th to 75th percentile) of survey respondents (N=141)

● Perceived library support for New Traditional students

● Perceived institutional support for New Traditional students

● UFLF (IPEDS) New Traditional enrollment profile

Percent

Figure 32. Top 100 Research-oriented Survey Respondents.

Our institution typology reflects a greater New Traditional character in the institutional enrollment profile for the top 100 Research-oriented respondents than is reflected in the survey data. As shown in Figure 32, our IPEDS-based assessment of the New Traditional profile for survey respondents is 63% greater than self-reported institutional profile. Consistent with the findings presented above, the top 100 Research-oriented institutions in the survey population perceive library support for New Traditional learners to be greater than overall institutional support. The difference between library and institutional support for New Traditional students is roughly comparable for the top 100 Research-oriented survey respondents and ARL respondents; this is partly explained by the fact that these segments overlap. Our typology-based segmentation has the benefit of providing a larger sample size for research-intensive institutions than is possible using ARL membership status alone. The net effect is a more representative view of library perceptions of institutional support for New Traditional students at research-intensive institutions.

Percent of perceived support for New Traditional students: Middle 50 percent (25th to 75th percentile) of survey respondents (N=141)

● Perceived library support for New Traditional students

● Perceived institutional support for New Traditional students

● UFLF (IPEDS) New Traditional enrollment profile

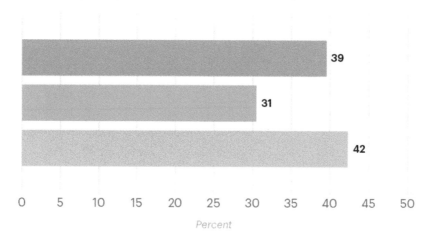

Figure 33. Middle 50% (25th to 75th percentile) of Survey Respondents (N-141).

Survey respondents from institutions in the mid-range of institutional emphasis on Research, Liberal Education and Career-directed learning perceive library attention to New Traditional students to be greater (by 26%) than institutional attention to these students. Our institution typology reflects a greater institutional orientation to New Traditional student demographics in mid-range institutions than is perceived by survey respondents from this segment. The institution typology reveals institutional attention to New Traditional students to be 35% greater than survey respondents' perceptions suggest.

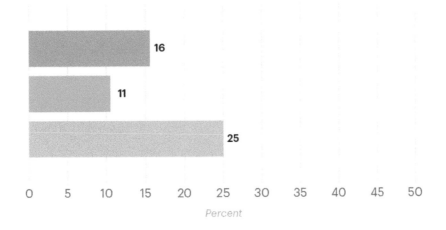

Percent of perceived support for New Traditional students: Top 100 Liberal Education-oriented survey respondents

● Perceived library support for New Traditional students

● Perceived institutional support for New Traditional students

● UFLF (IPEDS) New Traditional enrollment profile

Percent

Figure 34. Top 100 Liberal education-oriented Survey Respondents.

Looking beyond Oberlin Group, we see substantially higher self-reported institutional attention to New Traditional students among respondents from the top 100 Liberal Education institutions in our population. Among Oberlin Group respondents, the perceived institutional attention was a mere 2%, whereas the top 100 Liberal Education respondents reported an 11% share of institutional attention. However, institutional attention to New Traditional students in this segment was still well below what is revealed in our institution typology. As in other groups, respondents perceive library attention to New Traditional to be greater than overall institutional attention.

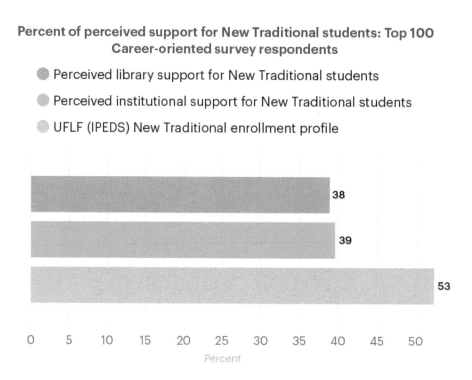

**Percent of perceived support for New Traditional students: Top 100
Career-oriented survey respondents**

● Perceived library support for New Traditional students

● Perceived institutional support for New Traditional students

● UFLF (IPEDS) New Traditional enrollment profile

Percent

Figure 35. Top 100 Career-oriented Survey Respondents.

In the top 100 Career-oriented institutions, survey respondents report institutional attention to New Traditional students to be substantially higher than was reported for the Top 100 Liberal Education or top 100 Research-oriented respondents. This is consistent with the difference revealed by our institution typology for these same groups: Career-directed institutions tend to serve a greater share of New Traditional students. A further interesting finding for the top 100 Career-oriented respondents is that they perceive library support for New Traditional students to be slightly less than institutional attention to this population. Career-directed institutions are the only segment in which respondents reported that institutional attention to New Traditional students exceeded library attention.

Percent of perceived support for New Traditional students: Top 100 New Traditional-oriented survey respondents

- Perceived library support for New Traditional students
- Perceived institutional support for New Traditional students
- UFLF (IPEDS) New Traditional enrollment profile

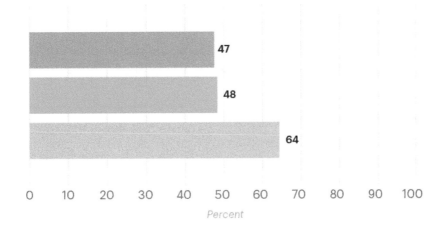

Figure 36. Top 100 New Traditional-oriented Survey Respondents.

Library directors in the institutions with the highest attention to New Traditional students perceive their institution's attention to New Traditional students to be greater (by 2%) than library support for this group of students. Notably, this, and the top 100 Career-oriented institutions are the only segments where this is true.

To summarize the key observations from our analysis of library and institutional attention to New Traditional student demographics, based on survey responses and our institution typology:

- Library directors generally perceive library support for New Traditional students to be greater than institutional support. This may reflect respondents' greater familiarity with library efforts to meet the needs of New Traditional students, compared to awareness of broader institutional efforts.

- Of the segments analyzed, only institutions with a high Career or high New Traditional institutional orientation perceive institutional attention to New Traditional students to be greater than library support for this population.

Academic library support for New Traditional student demographics is explored further in our summary of focus group interview findings.

Survey findings: library investments in key services areas

With respect to the key services areas, our survey questionnaire allows us to analyze how respondents believe they are currently allocating resources, how they expect their library to do so in five years' time, and what they believe an optimal allocation might be. For these questions, we specified that "Resources should include staffing, materials budget, space, other direct expenses, charged overhead, etc.—in other words, your entire budget, which includes all back-office functions." Our goal was to capture how library resources in total are, will be, and should be allocated across the key services areas. In this analysis, we examine aggregate findings, stratifications among member respondents of the ARL and Oberlin Group affinity groups, and stratifications among several categories derived from our typology.

Respondents were asked to allocate total library resources across the nine key service areas in our library services framework. With respect to the allocation of resources today, it is very clear that three key services areas dominate the others. Enable Academic Success and Facilitate Information Access each accounts for an average of 22 to 24% of reported resource allocation. Adding in Provide Study Space yields a total of 62%. No other services area approaches 10% of resources allocated.

Approximate share of resources devoted to each key services area today, all respondents

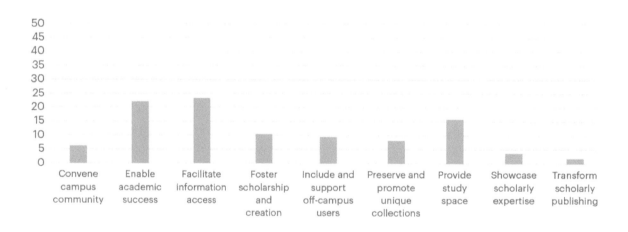

Figure 37. Approximate share of resources devoted to each key services area, today, all respondents.

Modest differences are observed when ARL and Oberlin stratifications are compared with the aggregate. For example, ARL respondents report devoting about five percentage points less to Enable Academic Success than the aggregate or the Oberlin Group. Both ARL and Oberlin respondents on average devoted less to Include and Support Off-Campus Users, while both provided more resources to Preserve and Promote Unique Collections.

Approximate share of resources devoted to each key services area today, affinity groups

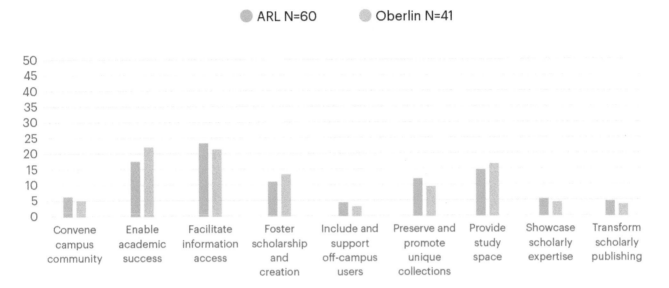

Figure 38. Approximate share of resources devoted to each key services area, today, affinity groups.

The typology-based groups offer relatively similar responses for most of the key services areas. Key differences can be found with respect to Support and Include Off-Campus Users, for which Liberal Arts and Research institutions are at less than half the share of resources as compared with Career institutions. By comparison, Research institutions devote on average a higher share of resources to Preserve and Promote Unique Collections, Showcase Scholarly Expertise, and Transform Scholarly Publishing.

Approximate share of resources devoted to each key services area today, typology groups

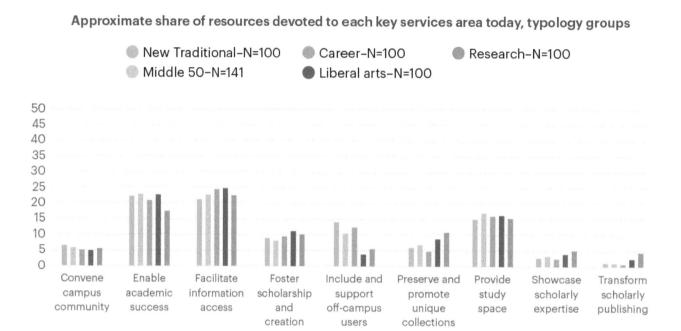

Figure 39. Approximate share of resources devoted to each key services area, today, typology groups.

Considering the optimal allocation of resources, respondents wish to see a lower allocation toward Facilitate Information Access (19.7%) than is currently the case today (23.5%). There is no area that is clearly prioritized for growth in an optimal allocation of resources.

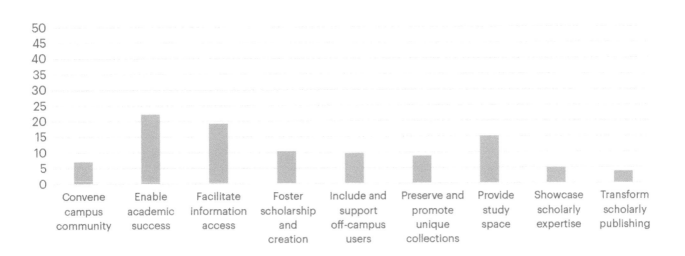

Approximate share of resources that should optimally be devoted to each key services area, all respondents

Figure 40. Approximate share of resources that should optimally be devoted to each key services area, all respondents.

The interest in reducing the allocation to Facilitate Information Access can be found not only within the aggregate but also among both ARL and Oberlin respondents. This service area is most pronounced as a reduction among ARL members. In turn, ARL members would optimally assign a higher level of resource to Transform Scholarly Publishing than would Oberlin respondents or the aggregate. Perhaps the most interesting reduction is planned for Provide Study Space, which we defined as "Provide physical spaces for academic collaboration, quiet study, and technology-enhanced instruction and/or learning." ARL institutions, in particular, seek to reduce the share of resources devoted to this function from 14.6% to 11.5% even as many large research library renovations provide additional user spaces by reducing on-site collections storage. Overall, while the optimal allocation differs somewhat between responding members of the two affinity groups, it is striking how similar their overall optimal allocations are to one another.

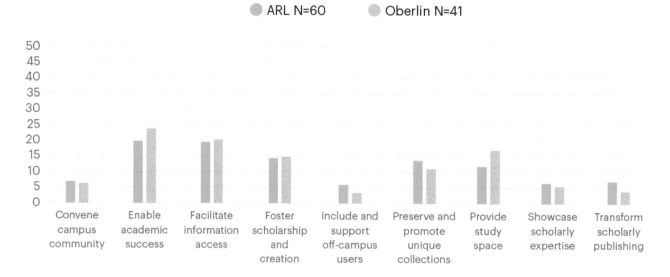

Figure 41. Approximate share of resources that should optimally be devoted to each key services area, affinity groups.

When measured by the typology groupings, we can observe further nuance in optimal resource allocations.[73] Notably, all five groupings would like to increase the share of resources devoted to Convene Campus Community, Showcase Scholarly Expertise, and Transform Scholarly Publishing. Granted, they allocate resources from somewhat different starting points and the rate of increase varies, but it is striking that these three key services areas will optimally capture a growing share of resources from members of all five groups. By contrast, there are three areas that would see optimally greater investment from Research and Liberal Arts institutions but at least modest optimal declines among Career institutions—Foster Scholarship and Creation and Preserve and Promote Unique Collections. Altogether, this analysis provides some clear evidence of where differing pressures of trends might be anticipated by typology-based institutions, even if it does not follow exactly the pattern that some observers might anticipate. Showcase Expertise and Transform Scholarly Publishing remain relevant, even at lower levels, at Career institutions.

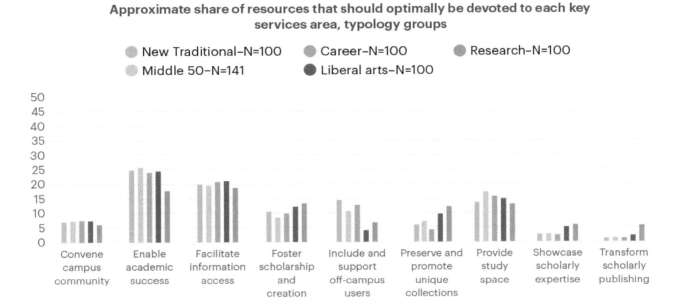

Figure 42. Approximate share of resources that should optimally be devoted to each key services area, typology groups.

Findings for anticipated resource allocations in five years from now map, at the aggregate level, very closely with the perceived optimal level.

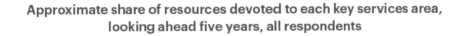

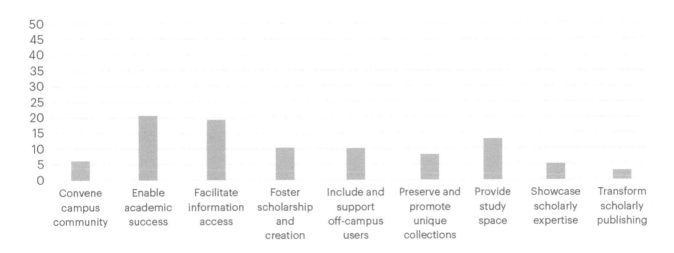

Figure 43. Approximate share of resources devoted to each key services area, looking ahead five years, all respondents.

There is one notable difference, however. Although ARL members believe the optimal level of resource allocation devoted to Enable Academic Success (18%) is just about exactly where it is today (17.9%), looking ahead five years, they expect to be able to devote a lower level of resources, only 15%, to this area. This is a curious finding and one that may merit further examination. A similar pattern for this item is observed for the New Traditional and Research stratifications in the typology groups.

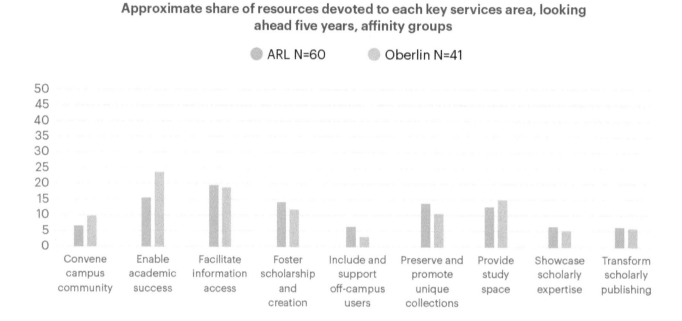

Figure 44. Approximate share of resources devoted to each key services area, looking ahead five years, affinity groups.

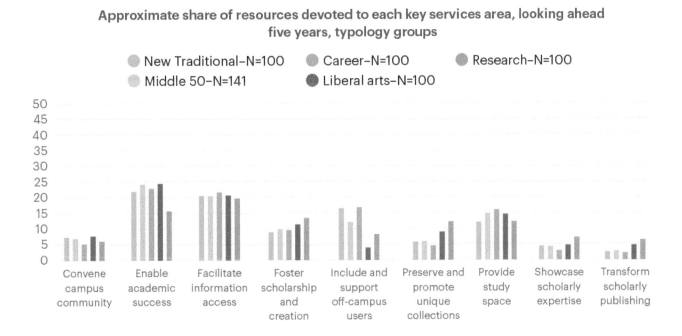

Figure 45. Approximate share of resources devoted to each key services area, looking ahead five years, typology groups.

In summary, our analysis of current and optimal library services directions reported by survey respondents reveals that:

- There is more alignment across library resource allocations today and future directions than there are substantial differences, whether measured by affinity groupings or typology groups.

- It is clear that some services areas are already "dialed up" or "dialed down" by responding libraries, in ways that align with, and perhaps are explained by, institutional groupings.

- There are some strikingly unexpected findings, such as the determination among ARL members that it would be optimal to reduce the share of resources devoted to Provide Study Space.

- Finally, our key services areas have explanatory power in a number of ways but also have their limitations. They broadly illustrate current resource allocation differences by institution type as well as anticipated change. But, at the same time, they also probably mask key differences at an individual service level, such as whether their notion of Transform Scholarly Publishing is more about research publication or student textbooks.

Focus group interview findings

We supplemented our survey analysis of library service directions with a series of focus groups designed to probe library directors' views on service needs in different institutional settings. Four focus group interviews were organized by OCLC Research between January and April, 2018. Each group was designed to include eight to ten library directors, selected from sub-populations of special interest. Invitations were extended to library directors representing a range of institution types, in order to test for notable variations in library service direction based on institutional setting.

The four groups included:

- Library directors from institutions with a declared focus on Liberal Education, as indicated by a formal affiliation with the American Association of Colleges and Universities (AAC&U), a nonprofit membership organization dedicated to "advanc[ing] the vitality and public standing of liberal education."[74] This focus group interview was scheduled to coincide with the annual meeting of AAC&U in Washington, DC, in January 2018. Twelve institutions were invited; ten participated in the meeting.

- Directors of US academic library consortia representing different segments of the higher education community. This focus group also included directors of two shared academic libraries, serving two or more colleges or universities. This meeting was organized in conjunction with the American Library Association (ALA) Midwinter Meeting in Denver, CO, in February 2018. Eighteen invitations were extended; nine institutions attended.

- Directors of academic libraries in the state of Colorado, representing a range of college and university types. This was a convenience sample, also organized in conjunction with the ALA Midwinter Meeting (2018). Fourteen invitations were extended; six institutions accepted and four ultimately participated.

- Directors of university libraries supporting institutions in the UIA, a coalition of public research universities "committed to increasing the number and diversity of college graduates in the United States."[75] This meeting was co-hosted by UIA library directors and organized in conjunction with the Coalition for Networked Information (CNI) meeting in San Diego, CA, in April 2018. All eleven UIA institutions were represented.

Each focus group interview included a brief overview of the University Futures, Library Futures project, followed by a review and discussion of institutional directions revealed by our institution typology. Participants received individualized radar charts, comparing educational directions at their parent institution with population and group averages. In a facilitated discussion, deans and directors shared local examples of library services offerings supporting Research, Liberal Education, and Career-directed Education directions at their institution. Beyond specific library services (e.g., research data management services or instructional design services), directors were invited to share information about specialized library staffing (a business librarian supporting student research of the job market, or a designated teaching/learning librarian, for instance) and library partnerships with other campus stakeholders (Office of Sponsored Research, Student Support Services unit, etc.). In a second exercise, directors reflected on library support for Traditional and New Traditional learners on their respective campuses.

A comparison of the average institutional educational directions for three of the focus groups is presented in figure 46. Averages for the consortium directors group are not included, as the compound average of multiple consortia is not representative of any given segment.

		Institution typology (N=25)			Survey responses (N=14)		
		Research	Liberal Education	Career-focused education	Research	Liberal Education	Career-focused education
Focus group	Liberal Education	0.22	0.58	0.20	0.16	0.59	0.25
	UIA	0.42	0.39	0.19	0.33	0.31	0.36
	Colorado academics	0.16	0.58	0.26	0.18	0.38	0.43

Figure 46. Focus Group Participants: Institution Typology vs. Survey Responses.

RECEPTION

Focus group participant responses to the institution typology and radar graphs fell into two main categories. The first type can be characterized as self-recognition and affirmation, in which individual participants readily recognized directions depicted in their institutional radar graph. One participant described the depiction of institutional directions as being "like getting your DNA profile," i.e., revelation of a core institutional identity. Another observed that the typology "speaks to the provost's priorities." The second category of participant responses can be characterized as doubt and skepticism, in which participants objected not to the typology or their institutional radar graphs, but to the feasibility of discussing or evaluating library services in the context of diverging educational priorities. Some participants objected to differentiating between library support for, e.g., Research and Liberal Education, or Traditional vs. New Traditional constituencies, arguing that library services are always designed with multiple audiences and institutional objectives in mind.

No focus group participants (nor any other discussants) took issue with the directions depicted, and even those who regarded the educational directions as "unnatural" categories for library services planning were able to identify areas of library investment that aligned more closely with one or at most two educational areas. One participant described the thought process as reverse-engineering past decisions to determine "were it not for [Stakeholder X], we would not have moved in this direction." Among consortium directors, in particular, there was a strong consensus that identifying opportunities for new service provision is especially challenging in groups of "differently shaped" institutions; typically, this results in a concentration of shared service provision around core services (content licensing, interlibrary loan, training and education) rather than innovation and experimentation. By contrast, in a consortium of university libraries with very similar institutional directions, the key challenge is in deciding which innovative new service to pursue.

UTILITY

The utility of the institution typology was recognized by library directors in each focus group. Directors were especially interested in using the typology to identify peer organizations, namely academic institutions with similar educational directions (as reflected in the institution typology and radar graphs) and/or similar enrollment profiles (Traditional/New Traditional distribution). This provides powerful, if anecdotal, evidence of the importance of institutional isomorphism in shaping expectations and establishing norms for library service models. Several directors observed that identifying "similarly shaped" peers could be useful in building partnerships for cooperative sourcing and service development. The interest in identifying potential partners was equally strong for our first-dimension analysis (institutional educational directions) and our secondary dimension analysis (enrollment profile). Many directors acknowledged that adapting existing services, or developing new ones to meet the needs of New Traditional students was a growing priority, and expressed a desire to find institutions facing similar challenges.

In the weeks and months following focus group interviews, we received several requests from participants interested in using the institution typology for local strategic planning. For example, one library director notified us that he had used the typology and institutional radar graph to discuss institutional priorities and library alignment with the university's provost.

FINDINGS: LIBRARY SERVICE DIRECTIONS

As noted above, focus group participants were asked to identify existing or planned library support related to each of the educational directions in our institution typology, and later participated in a facilitated discussion of library support for New Traditional student populations. These exercises and discussions produced a broad evidence base of information about library service directions in a wide range of institutional settings, based on input from 34 directors. Here we summarize a number of high-level findings.

A notable pattern emerged in each and across all the focus groups: participants could readily identify specific and often similar library services, staffing, and stakeholder partnerships intended to support Research or Liberal education. As our survey findings also suggest, these institutional directions are supported by a robust array of specialized library service offerings, dedicated staffing, and usually well-established stakeholder partnerships with other campus units. Examples for Research support include research data management support, virtual computing lab, high-performance computing, research data librarians, GIS specialists, and partnerships with graduate centers, research centers, etc. Examples for Liberal Education support include writing labs in libraries, textbook collections, museum exhibition design, online learning librarians, technology librarians, archives and special collections librarians, teaching and learning librarians, and partnerships with student success and first-year student success centers.

By contrast, there was little agreement about what constitutes adequate (never mind excellent) library support for Career-directed Education programs. This finding is consistent with the analysis of survey results, which revealed a gap between perceived institutional and library directions related to Career-directed Education. For some focus groups participants, library support for this area was a lower priority because the college or university had limited educational activity that was explicitly oriented toward immediate professional advancement. But for others, notably directors supporting institutions with a strong directional emphasis on Career-directed Education, there was a tangible sense of frustration that the library had only limited engagement with professions-oriented academic programs. One director acknowledged that career attainment is a primary focus of the institution the library serves, and described several thwarted efforts to cultivate partnerships with other stakeholders (Career Services unit, internship partners from the local business community), who felt the library had little to offer. Library directors from UIA member institutions emphasized that UIA's focus on increasing the number and diversity of college graduates has resulted in greater institutional attention to educational outcomes beyond graduation. In this context, library support for student success is understood to encompass post-graduation achievement, as well as retention and graduation rates. While several participants identified Career Services as a key campus stakeholder, none cited specific examples of successful library partnerships with this organizational unit.

The fact that our focus group interviews revealed no strong examples of positive library engagement with Career Services units does not, in itself, provide evidence of a general gap in academic library attention or service innovation in this area. The research team's background investigation identified several examples of college and university libraries that offer customized training and research services to assist students with identifying potential employers, support for e-portfolio software implementation, or provide space for Career Services professionals within the library. Other researchers have examined the opportunities for library engagement with Career Services and offer concrete examples of impactful library programs.[76]

The dearth of engagement-oriented library services for Career-directed education was lamented by several directors, who contrasted the continued reliance on collections-based support (e.g., library-licensed test preparation resources, online skill-building tutorials) for professional education with the growing emphasis on expertise services and workflow support for research, teaching, and learning elsewhere in the library. One university library director reported on a successful initiative to have the library take the lead in implementing an e-portfolio solution designed to support student learning assessment as well as providing a virtual portfolio of academic and co-curricular activities that students can promote to prospective employers. This was the perhaps the most innovative example of an engagement-oriented, Career-directed library support services that emerged from the focus group interviews.

Yet, as the library director acknowledged, the success of this library-led e-portfolio initiative was due in part to a serendipitous combination of software engineering skills and fortuitous slack in staff capacity that enabled the library to step forward as a project lead. Academic libraries in smaller institutions might find it difficult to emulate this model. It is nonetheless intriguing to consider a scenario in which libraries assume a greater role in managing teaching and learning outputs aggregated in e-portfolio systems, along with research outputs aggregated in institutional repositories. Among other things, this could position the library as a key partner in institutional reputation management.

As the focus group interviews progressed, a notable pattern emerged. Library directors from institutions of all types reported significant challenges in characterizing and communicating the value and impact of library activities on student enrollment (are institutional recruitment targets being met?), retention (are enrolled students persisting in their studies?), and success (do students progress toward graduation, employment or further educational pathways?). Without exception, participants in the group interviews acknowledged that the library is increasingly expected to characterize its "value add" to the college or university in terms of positive gains and outcomes, in addition to efficient management of costs. As is amply documented in a recent ACRL/OCLC report on academic library impact, institutional assessment of libraries is increasingly framed in terms of the missions and goals of the parent college or university.[77]

The report's authors specifically call out the need for closer alignment of university and library expectations regarding the library's role(s) in student learning and success outcomes, and improved communication between library administrators and other campus stakeholders.[78] Other researchers have proposed that library administrators should more systematically approach stakeholder communication in terms of reciprocal value propositions.[79] This is a potentially fruitful area for further collaborative research to identify, generalize, and scale innovative approaches to communicating library impact not just on research and teaching, but also on student engagement.

Another striking finding from our focus group interviews was the importance of consortial partnerships in developing or sourcing (purchasing or licensing) solutions that supported one or another institutional need. Notably, library directors in institutions that were transforming educational programming (launching new doctoral programs to enhance the university's research reputation, or diversifying into online professional programs) acknowledged that expanding, or in some instances pivoting, library services toward new institutional needs made collaborative partnerships increasingly important. Several directors identified consortial collections (resource-sharing networks, as well as shared library storage and "shared print" partnerships) as a critical component of their Research support activities. Others pointed to the importance of consortial support for Open Educational Resources and e-textbook licensing as an aid in demonstrating the library's commitment to reducing costs for students, as well as supporting faculty innovation.

Some participants acknowledged that consortial partnerships that were forged to support one area of need (e.g., content licensing) are not necessarily a good fit for areas of emerging university need (supporting a new executive education program, or new global campus initiative, for example). Interestingly, several directors speculated that ad hoc partnerships among institutions "with a similar shape"—i.e., similar institutional directions—might become more important as the educational landscape continues to diversify. A similar observation was voiced by consortium directors, who acknowledged that finding common ground for collaboration action in large and heterogeneous groups is becoming more challenging as libraries reconfigure themselves to support sometimes divergent institutional interests. In an increasingly engagement- and services-oriented library environment, consortia must specialize their offer, forcing a difficult choice between leveraging economies of scope and scale.[80]

LIBRARY SUPPORT FOR NEW TRADITIONAL STUDENTS

Among our focus groups, library directors from our Colorado convenience sample and UIA institutions had the most to say about New Traditional student populations. These directors were knowledgeable about the life circumstances of their students, citing specific examples about the work/education balance of students, providing statistics on the share of first-generation students and traditionally marginalized populations, and drawing explicit connections to services and space needs in the library. For example, directors reported on efforts to repurpose library collections space to support meditation and prayer spaces (including appropriate accommodations for wudu ablutions), lactation rooms, family study spaces, and the like. Some directors described adjusting library service hours to accommodate the needs of working and commuter students; others reported on library anxiety experienced by returning adult students and the particular challenges of building rapport and trust between public services staff and, e.g., returning military veterans or adult students pursuing professional certificate and masters programs. Several directors reported that they are re-examining library work-study positions as a mechanism for building bridges with New Traditional students, providing meaningful "career-ready" work experience and aligning library work assignments with High Impact Practices prioritized by their colleges and universities.

Figure 47 compares the average New Traditional score for each focus group based on our institution typology and survey responses from these same institutions. Notably, the perceptions of Colorado academic library directors are quite close to the New Traditional profile revealed by our typology. This would seem to confirm their more intimate knowledge of the student demographics served by their institutions, as well as closer personal knowledge of student life circumstances.[81] Consortium focus group scores are not reported, as it was not feasible to compute an aggregate profile for the largest consortia. The consortium focus group also had comparatively little to say regarding New Traditional students or relevant library services. This is unsurprising, given that consortium leaders have typically limited contact with the campus communities served by their member libraries, and, hence, limited insights on the student enrollment profile (beyond its overall size).

| New Traditional enrollment profile | | |
Institution typology (N=25)	Survey responses (N=15)
Focus group — Liberal Education	0.43	0.24
Focus group — UIA	0.36	0.21
Focus group — Colorado academics	0.57	0.52

Figure 47. Focus Groups: New Traditional Enrollment Profile.

While focus group participants acknowledged that their institutions serve a heterogenous student population, it was not evident that library directors in Liberal Education institutions were familiar with many New Traditional students. Possibly, this is due to significant online enrollment of New Traditional students in some of these institutions, which reduces their physical presence (and visibility) on campus or in the library. Another explanation could be that highly exclusive institutions tend to admit a relatively Traditional student population. Interestingly, during the discussion with this group, it emerged among several participants that the New Traditional student that they were thinking of was middle-aged students, specifically women and military veterans were mentioned, returning to higher education after years away from it, or entering higher education for the first time in mid-life, likely for their personal enrichment (but notably not for work-related training).

In this chapter, we reviewed the methods and findings from our survey of academic library directors and focus group interviews with directors from segments within the project population. The survey data and fieldwork provide the foundation for conclusions developed in Chapter 6. Here, we highlight a few of the most notable findings from our research:

- Our survey revealed that library directors generally perceive current academic library directions to be closely aligned with institutional educational priorities.

- Despite reporting close alignment of library and institutional priorities, directors acknowledged that an "optimal" allocation of library budget (one that maximizes the fit between library and institutional directions) would look somewhat different. There appears to be a broad consensus that library resources should be redirected from collections-centric "information access" activity toward other areas (improving support for scholarly communication, investments in institutional and researcher reputation management, highlighting distinctive collections, etc.).

- In general, library directors perceive institutional directions to be somewhat less differentiated along Research, Liberal Education and Career directions than is borne out in our analysis of IPEDS data; i.e., they perceive the college or university interests to be more evenly distributed across these directions.

- Directors generally believe the library places a greater emphasis on supporting flexible modes of education than the university as a whole. However, the very small cohort of academic library directors from Colorado generally reported that the parent institution has a slightly greater emphasis on support for New Traditional students. Interestingly, our institution typology and survey results both indicate that these institutions do have a majority New Traditional enrollment profile.

- There is limited consensus on appropriate models of library support for Career-directed Education.

Chapter 6: Concluding Reflections

The research presented in this report is intended to clarify how changes in the US higher education environment are likely to shape the future of academic libraries. In our introductory chapter, we described the highly competitive environment of higher education and predicted that institutions would seek to further differentiate themselves to capture more value in emerging higher education markets.

Using statistical data on US higher education institutions, we developed a framework for evaluating institutional educational activity along three different, but not mutually, exclusive directions: doctoral-level research (in which universities compete for global research reputation as well as research funding); baccalaureate education in the arts and sciences (where colleges and universities compete for tuition revenue); and career-directed programs producing "work ready" credentials in a specific discipline or profession (where competition is focused on perceptions of "value for money").

Additionally, we considered the variable institutional attention to serving the growing educational market for New Traditional students. We imagined a world in which libraries would "dial up" or dial down" certain service offerings, to optimize the fit between library services and institutional priorities with respect to educational directions and enrollment profile.

What we discovered in applying our typology to the narrowly scoped population in our project, is that institutional identities do tend to cluster around distinctive educational directions, with a small number of extreme outliers defining the "outer reaches." The most intensive research universities and selective residential liberal arts colleges continue to focus on their traditional missions and compete more intensely for a diminishing number of Traditional undergraduate students. Other institutions—regional universities, but also many smaller colleges—are adapting to serve new markets for professions-oriented baccalaureate, master's, and certificate programs.

Dwindling numbers of Traditional, full-time students between the ages of 18 and 25 have motivated these institutions to design programs that appeal to other populations. Online and hybrid courses have been created in response to the students' needs for flexible scheduling. Programs of study have been designed in partnership with regional businesses to address workforce issues. More students are encouraged to pursue pathways that maximize efficiency in credit-generating coursework and lead to more direct employment opportunities. Course schedules are created to allow maximum opportunities for students to finish their degrees in four years, as a way of reducing the cost of higher education.

Changing institutional missions and priorities naturally affect the services that students require for their success. How are libraries responding to these changes? Our research suggests that library directors are cognizant of broader institutional interests and educational directions (e.g., a research university with significant career-directed educational programming, a college with a dominant liberal education orientation, and so on), and generally confident that the library's strategic direction is congruent with institutional interests. Library directors at Research universities are more focused on research services of the library than their counterparts; Liberal Arts college library directors are more focused on equipping their campus population with library literacy skills. Interestingly, ARL directors are more inclined to rate research orientation lower than the typology we defined, probably because there has been a surge in prioritizing undergraduate student success in the intensive research institutions. In all cases, library directors believe that their current strategic directions are closely aligned with their institutions' strategic directions.

It is in the group of institutions that are not categorized as intensive research or liberal arts institutions that we see more of a gap in perceived need and services offered. Library directors acknowledge a gap between Career-directed Education and library support for this activity. The challenge for these libraries, and to a lesser extent for all libraries, is to learn more about what the New Traditional students require to be successful and determine ways in which library services can be configured to meet those needs.

Library directors in the Career-directed institutions perceive library support for New Traditional learners to be greater than institutional support. Since we did not query institutions about the support services provided beyond the library, we are not in a position to judge the relative level of service provision, but higher education literature suggests that the needs of New Traditional students go far beyond the ability to identify, assess, and access information sources. Needs of these students range from more customized advising, to access to the latest technology, to spaces and places to study that accommodate families and are available around the clock. These students may need financial planning assistance, advice about successful study habits, support services to address food and/or housing insecurity, or general orientation services for first-generation students. Since time management is always an issue for the New Traditional student, is consolidating all of these services in a single place—the library—worth considering?

As more hybrid and online courses are offered in all segments of higher education, is the library equipped to provide high-quality services to the students who do not use the physical facility, as well as to those who do? What changes are required in terms of staffing and staff training?

As we looked at the responses of library directors of the different types of institutions, we saw more similarities than differences in their resource allocations across the key services areas framework that we developed. That is, regardless of institution type or affinity group, on average, library director respondents report devoting the most resources to the core functions of enabling academic success, facilitating information access, and providing study space.

Still, there were noteworthy differences in resource allocations and anticipated future allocations. Research institutions, with their wide range of user communities and priorities, devote a smaller share of resources compared with other institution types to enabling student success. Career and New Traditional institutions devote a higher share of resources than do others to supporting and including off-campus users, which is reflected in their student populations and educational delivery models. Research and Liberal Arts institutions devote a higher share of resources than do others to preserving and promoting unique collections, a reminder that special collections initiatives resonate differently across institution types.

Directionally, the aggregate of responding directors and almost all the affinity and typology groups we analyzed are interested in reducing the share of their resource investment in facilitating information access. This suggests the broad recognition that in a digital and increasingly open environment, this work may decline in amount if not in value. Directors seem to envision doing so with at least some increase in the resources devoted to transforming scholarly publishing, most strikingly at ARL member institutions. There are some differing directions based on our typology analysis that suggest some continuing divergence between research and liberal arts institutions as compared with career and other institution types. While not dramatic in nature, they do suggest that directors are sensitive to the differing needs of their parent institutions in their planning for resource allocation.

Key takeaways

This project has been important in underlining how institutional differences play into library differences and in refining our view of institutional differences. Here are some important contributions of this work:

- **The institutional typology developed here has considerable analytical and heuristic power.** Comparing typology-based segmentation to existing affinity groups, we find that our institution typology reliably characterizes known institution types with the significant added advantage that the typology can be used to test institutional directions for colleges and universities not formally affiliated with affinity groups (ARL, Oberlin Group, etc.). This is potentially important in identifying relevant peer groups for benchmarking or collaborative partnerships. We believe that this is a major contribution of this work and **already has generated considerable interest among libraries and library groups who wish to factor institutional type into discussion.**

- The library key services areas we propose here also have explanatory power in a number of ways. They work well to illustrate current resource allocation differences by institution type as well as anticipated change in some broad categories of service. At the same time, they also probably mask key differences at an individual service level, such as whether their notion of Transform Scholarly Publishing is more about research publication or student textbooks. This is not surprising as we are seeing the "classic" library divisions/services morph, without yet having been replaced by a constantly agreed set of new categories. We believe that **further work to refine and validate services areas would be valuable, as libraries look at comparative planning, assessment, and organizational design.**

- Our hypothesis was that as universities diversified their educational offer, libraries would adapt services based on institutional fit. Our work has confirmed that this is happening. In fact, **survey respondents by and large believe that the institutional typology is a good indicator of their institutional strategies and that they are already aligning services with their home institution.** The majority believe that their allocation to services areas within five years will bring library services even closer to the optimum institutional strategy fit. Accordingly, it is clear that some services areas are already "dialed up" or "dialed down" by responding library, in ways that align with, and perhaps are explained by, institutional groupings.

- However, differences in the mix of service area allocations across institutional types are not as pronounced as we might have expected. There are some interesting findings when we consider the optimal allocation of resources across services areas. **Most notable is the interest in reducing allocations to Facilitate Information Access, which is in line with more broadly observed shift from collections to services.**

- **An important contribution of this work has been to focus on the role of libraries in supporting university goals around preparing students for careers and in supporting New Traditional students.** Results show that this is an important area for many libraries and they recognize its importance to their universities. However, how to do this effectively is not widely agreed. This also highlights how little examined in the library literature, and at conferences, library services in this area are, despite increased public (and policy) attention to how universities are adapting to the future of work, the impact of automation on labor markets, and so on.[82] This was supported by discussion at the focus groups, where it also was suggested that staff at Career-oriented institutions have less capacity for broader professional participation and research. This is an area where more work would be of great benefit to the profession generally.

Based on the work and results presented here, we think that further work in these areas would be of broad interest:

- We see a variety of applications for the institutional typology supporting analysis and identification of library groups and directions. One area to emerge in discussion with libraries has been in profiling consortia, in terms of constituent institutional profiles. Interest in a "peer finder" application also has been voiced by a number of institutions.

- Refinement and validation of key library services areas. It is clear that we are transitioning to a new service portfolio, focused on student success and retention, research support, and community engagement. The framework presented here maps well onto service directions but can be refined and validated further.

- Patterns and models of service for supporting institutional goals around career-preparedness and support for New Traditional students have emerged as an important area requiring further investigation.

- Library interest in assessment is high, which is natural given changes in research and learning behaviors and institutional expectations of the library. The framework presented here may support a more directed assessment discussion.

The research presented in this report suggests that increasing diversification in the higher education enterprise is acknowledged by library administrators and recognized as a potential challenge, notably with respect to library support for career-directed education and responsiveness to the needs of New Traditional student demographics. We applaud the efforts that library leaders are making to evaluate and respond to changing institutional needs, and strongly urge research, service, and professional library organizations (including our own) to assist in identifying and promoting strategies and practices that improve the alignment of academic library strategy with emerging, and diverging, institutional priorities across the higher education landscape.

Notes

1. Paul DiMaggio and Walter W. Powell. 1983. "The Iron Cage Revisited: Collective Rationality and Institutional Isomorphism in Organizational Fields." *American Sociological Review* 48, no. 2: 147-60; Kevin Carey. 2015. *The End of College: Creating the Future of Learning and the University of Everywhere*. New York: Riverhead Books; and Michael M. Crow and William B. Dabars. 2015. *Designing the New American University*. Baltimore, Maryland: Johns Hopkins University Press. (See, e.g., the discussion on p. 118).

2. Michael M. Crow and William B. Dabars. 2015. *Designing the New American University*. Baltimore, Maryland: Johns Hopkins University Press.

3. Throughout this report we use the phrase "library services" to describe a broad range of library activities, including but not limited to collections management or facilitating information access. A general shift in focus of library services from collections to engagement is widely acknowledged in research literature; however, traditional conceptions of library services focused on collections management persist. Recent research by OCLC colleagues has revealed important differences in how library staff and academic administrators perceive and communicate the value of library services. Connaway et al. recommend that library leaders use more specific descriptive terms (e.g., programs, exhibits) to describe the range of value-creating activities that the library supports and link those activities more explicitly to specific institutional priorities. See Lynn Silipigni Connaway, William Harvey, Vanessa Kitzie, and Stephanie Mikitish. 2017. *Academic Library Impact: Improving Practice and Essential Areas to Research*. Chicago, Illinois: Association of College and Research Libraries. http://www.ala.org/acrl/sites/ala.org.acrl/files/content/publications/whitepapers/academiclib.pdf.

4. Evan Farber. 1974. "College Librarians and the University-library Syndrome." In Lyle. *The Academic Library: Essays in Honor of Guy R. Lyle*. Edited by Evan Ira Farber and Ruth Walling, 12–23. Metuchen, N.J: Scarecrow Press.

5. While many factors have contributed to the redefinition of academic library quality, it is worth calling out the ongoing shift toward shared management of print inventory as an important influence. As a growing number of institutions, including major research universities, implement "shared print" approaches, the notion that a vast local inventory is a hallmark of excellence, is waning. See, e.g., Bob Kieft. 2010. "A College Library, Its Print Monograph Collection and the New Information Ecology." *Against the Grain* 22, no. 5: 28-30. https://doi.org/10.7771/2380-176X.5643.

6. Lorcan Dempsey and Constance Malpas. 2018. "Academic Library Futures in a Diversified University System." In *Higher Education in the Era of the Fourth Industrial Revolution*. Edited by Nancy W. Gleason. Singapore: Palgrave Macmillan. https://doi.org/10.1007/978-981-13-0194-0_4.

7. A related issue here is the role of Library and Information Schools in normalizing standards of excellence in library education and administration. For an exploration of how the disciplinary identity of library and information science is shaped by institutional directions, see MaryBeth Walpole. 2000. "Under Construction: Identity and Isomorphism in the Merger of a Library and Information Science School and an Education School." *The Library Quarterly* 70, no. 4 (October): 423-45. https://doi.org/10.1086/603216.

8. Martin Trow. 1974. "Problems in the Transition from Elite to Mass Higher Education." In *Policies for Higher Education: General Report on the Conference on Future Structures of Post-Secondary Education*, 55–101. Paris: OECD, quoted in John Brennan, Vassiliki Papatsiba, Sofia Branco Sousa, and David M. Hoffman. 2016. "Diversity of Higher Education Institutions in Networked Knowledge Societies: A Comparative Examination." In *Re-becoming Universities? Higher Education Institutions in Networked Knowledge Societies*, 115–39. Dordrecht: Springer Netherlands. https://doi.org/10.1007/978-94-017-7369-0_5.

9. John Brennan, Vassiliki Papatsiba, Sofia Branco Sousa, and David M. Hoffman. 2016. "Diversity of Higher Education Institutions in Networked Knowledge Societies: A Comparative Examination." In *Re-becoming Universities? Higher Education Institutions in Networked Knowledge Societies*, 115–39. Dordrecht: Springer Netherlands. https://doi.org/10.1007/978-94-017-7369-0_5.

10. T. Becher and M. Kogan. 1992. *Process and Structure in Higher Education*, 2nd ed. London: Routledge; and B. Clark. 1983. *The Higher Education System. Academic Organization in Cross-national Perspective*. Berkley: University of California Press, quoted in John Brennan, Vassiliki Papatsiba, Sofia Branco Sousa, and David M. Hoffman. 2016. "Diversity of Higher Education Institutions in Networked Knowledge Societies: A Comparative Examination." In *Re-becoming Universities? Higher Education Institutions in Networked Knowledge Societies*, 115–39. Dordrecht: Springer Netherlands. https://doi.org/10.1007/978-94-017-7369-0_5.

11. Brian Prescott. 2011. "Thinking Anew About Institutional Taxonomies." Paper presented at the Mapping Broad-Access Higher Education Conference, Stanford University, 1-2 December 2011, Stanford, CA. http://cepa.stanford.edu/conference-papers/thinking-anew-about-institutional-taxonomies.

12. Ibid.

13. Ibid.

14. National Science Foundation. 2012. "Carnegie Classifications." Technical Notes. Updated 5 April 2012. https://sestat.nsf.gov/docs/carnegie.html; and Indiana University. 2016. "The Carnegie Classification of Institutions of Higher Education." News and Announcements, About the Carnegie Classification®. Accessed 27 July 2016. http://carnegieclassifications.iu.edu/.

15. National Science Foundation. 2012. "Carnegie Classifications." Technical Notes. Updated 5 April 2012. https://sestat.nsf.gov/docs/carnegie.html.

16. Ibid.

17. Indiana University 2016. "The Carnegie Classification of Institutions of Higher Education 2015 Edition." Indiana University Center for Postsecondary Research. http://carnegieclassifications.iu.edu/methodology/basic.php.

18. Steven Brint. 2013. "A Priori and Empirical Approaches to the Classification of Higher Education Institutions: The United States Case." Pensamiento Educativo: Revista de Investigación Educacional Latinoamericana 50 (1): 96–114. https://doi.org/10.7764/PEL.50.1.2013.8.

19. Martin Ruef and Manish Nag. 2015. "The Classification of Organizational Forms: Theory and Application to the Field of Higher Education." In *Remaking College: The Changing Ecology of Higher Education*, edited by Michael W. Kirst and Mitchell L Stevens, 84–109. Stanford, CA: Stanford University Press. https://www.researchgate.net/publication/303297642_The_Classification_of_Organizational_Forms_Theory_and_Application_to_the_Field_of_Higher_Education.

20. Steven Brint. 2013. "A Priori and Empirical Approaches to the Classification of Higher Education Institutions: The United States Case." *Pensamiento Educativo: Revista de Investigación Educacional Latinoamericana* 50 (1): 96–114. https://doi.org/10.7764/PEL.50.1.2013.8.

21. Ibid.

22. Francis Oakely. 1997. "The Elusive Academic Profession: Complexity and Change." *Daedalus* 126: 47; and John Thelin. 2004. *A History of American Higher Education*. Baltimore, MD: Johns Hopkins Press, quoted in Martin Ruef and Manish Nag. 2015. "The Classification of Organizational Forms: Theory and Application to the Field of Higher Education." In *Remaking College: The Changing Ecology of Higher Education*, edited by Michael W. Kirst and Mitchell L Stevens, 84–109. Stanford, CA: Stanford University Press. https://www.researchgate.net/publication/303297642_The_Classification_of_Organizational_Forms_Theory_and_Application_to_the_Field_of_Higher_Education.

23. Howard Aldrich and Martin Ruef. 2006. *Organizations Evolving*. 2nd ed. London: Sage, 128, quoted in Martin Ruef and Manish Nag. 2015. "The Classification of Organizational Forms: Theory and Application to the Field of Higher Education." In *Remaking College: The Changing Ecology of Higher Education*, edited by Michael W. Kirst and Mitchell L Stevens, 84–109. Stanford, CA: Stanford University Press. https://www.researchgate.net/publication/303297642_The_Classification_of_Organizational_Forms_Theory_and_Application_to_the_Field_of_Higher_Education.

24. Jerome Karabel. 2005. *The Chosen: The Hidden History of Admission at Harvard, Yale and Princeton*. Boston, MA: Houghton Mifflin, quoted in Martin Ruef and Manish Nag. 2015. "The Classification of Organizational Forms: Theory and Application to the Field of Higher Education." In *Remaking College: The Changing Ecology of Higher Education*, edited by Michael W. Kirst and Mitchell L Stevens, 84–109. Stanford, CA: Stanford University Press. https://www.researchgate.net/publication/303297642_The_Classification_of_Organizational_Forms_Theory_and_Application_to_the_Field_of_Higher_Education.

25. Patricia J. Gumport, Maria Iannozzi, Susan Shaman, and Robert Zemsky. 1997. *The United States Country Report: Trends in Higher Education from Massification to Post-Massification*. Stanford, CA: National Center for Postsecondary Improvement, 13. https://web.stanford.edu/group/ncpi/documents/pdfs/1-04_massification.pdf, quoted in Indiana University. 2016. "The Carnegie Classification of Institutions of Higher Education." News and Announcements, About the Carnegie Classification®. Accessed 27 July 2016. http://carnegieclassifications.iu.edu/.

26. Steven Brint. 2013. "A Priori and Empirical Approaches to the Classification of Higher Education Institutions: The United States Case." Pensamiento Educativo: Revista de Investigación Educacional Latinoamericana 50 (1): 96–114. https://doi.org/10.7764/PEL.50.1.2013.8.

27. Ibid., 9

28. Ibid.

29. Michael T. Hannan. 2010. "Partiality of Memberships in Categories and Audiences." *Annual Review of Sociology* 36: 159–181. https://doi.org/10.1146/annurev-soc-021610-092336, quoted in Martin Ruef and Manish Nag. 2015. "The Classification of Organizational Forms: Theory and Application to the Field of Higher Education." In *Remaking College: The Changing Ecology of Higher Education*, edited by Michael W. Kirst and Mitchell L Stevens, 84–109. Stanford, CA: Stanford University Press. https://www.researchgate.net/publication/303297642_The_Classification_of_Organizational_Forms_Theory_and_Application_to_the_Field_of_Higher_Education.

30. Steven Brint. 2013. "A Priori and Empirical Approaches to the Classification of Higher Education Institutions: The United States Case." Pensamiento Educativo: Revista de Investigación Educacional Latinoamericana 50 (1): 96–114. https://doi.org/10.7764/PEL.50.1.2013.8.

31. Anya Kamenetz. 2015. "DIY U: Higher Education Goes Hybrid." In *Remaking College: The Changing Ecology of Higher Education*, edited by Michael W. Kirst and Mitchell L. Stevens, 39–60. Stanford, CA: Stanford University Press; Use of New Traditional to describe the changing student enrollment profile is increasingly prevalent in the general higher education press as well. See, e.g., Autumn Arnett. 2017. "Mincing Words: Nontraditional is the New Traditional" *Education Dive* (news), *Industry Dive* 29 September 2017. https://www.educationdive.com/news/linguistics-nontraditional-is-the-new-traditional/506114/; Steve Fireng. 2016. "The Rise of the Nontraditional Student, or Is It the 'New Traditional Student'?" *CEO Keys* (blog), *Keypath Education*. 29 August 2016. https://keypathedu.com/blog/2016/08/29/rise-nontraditional-student-or-it-new-traditional-student; and Rob Jenkins. 2012. "The New 'Traditional Student.'" *The Chronicle of Higher Education* (Advice section), 15 October 2012. https://www.chronicle.com/article/The-New-Traditional-on/135012.

32. NCES. 2015. "Digest of Education Services." List of 2015 Digest Tables. https://nces.ed.gov/programs/digest/2015menu_tables.asp. (OCLC's calculations)

33. For further information on older students, see Goldie Blumenstyk. 2018. *The Adult Student: The Population Colleges—and the Nation—can't Afford to Ignore*. [Washington, D.C.]: Chronicle of Higher Education.

34. NCES. 2016. "Table 301.20. Historical Summary of Faculty, Enrollment, Degrees Conferred, and Finances in Degree-Granting Postsecondary Institutions: Selected Years, 1869-70 through 2013-14." National Center for Education Statistics. https://nces.ed.gov/programs/digest/d15/tables/dt15_301.20.asp.

35. NCES. 2016. "Table 303.10. Total Fall Enrollment in Degree-Granting Postsecondary Institutions, by Attendance Status, Sex of Student, and Control of Institution: Selected Years, 1947 through 2025." National Center for Education Statistics. https://nces.ed.gov/programs/digest/d15/tables/dt15_303.10.asp?current=yes.

36. NCES. 2015. "Table 303.40. Total Fall Enrollment in Degree-Granting Postsecondary Institutions, by Attendance Status, Sex, and Age: Selected Years, 1970 through 2024." National Center for Education Statistics. https://nces.ed.gov/programs/digest/d14/tables/dt14_303.40.asp. (OCLC's calculations)

37. NCES. 2015. Digest of Education Services. https://nces.ed.gov/programs/digest/2015menu_tables.asp. (OCLC's calculations)

38. Terms for race in this publication are used according to the US Census Bureau standards. They "must adhere to the 1997 Office of Management and Budget (OMB) standards on race and ethnicity which guide the Census Bureau in classifying written responses to the race question." See their website for full definitions: "About Race" https://www.census.gov/topics/population/race/about.html.

39. NCES. 2015. "Table 302.60. Percentage of 18- to 24-Year-Olds Enrolled in Degree-Granting Postsecondary Institutions, by Level of Institution and Sex and Race/ethnicity of Student: 1970 through 2014." National Center for Education Statistics. https://nces.ed.gov/programs/digest/d15/tables/dt15_302.60.asp. As a consequence of this scoping decision, community colleges are excluded from our study. Community colleges are an important sector and may be the subject of future work exploring the application of our model to a broader share of the US higher education sector.

40. NCES. 2016. "Table 302.30. Percentage of Recent High School Completers Enrolled in 2-Year and 4-Year Colleges, by Income Level: 1975 through 2015." National Center for Education Statistics. https://nces.ed.gov/programs/digest/d16/tables/dt16_302.30.asp.

41. Pew Research Center. 2016. "America's Shrinking Middle Class: A Close Look at Change within Metropolitan Areas." http://assets.pewresearch.org/wp-content/uploads/sites/3/2016/05/Middle-Class-Metro-Areas-FINAL.pdf.

42. NCES. 2015. "Table 303.40. Total Fall Enrollment in Degree-Granting Postsecondary Institutions, by Attendance Status, Sex, and Age: Selected Years, 1970 through 2024." National Center for Education Statistics. https://nces.ed.gov/programs/digest/d14/tables/dt14_303.40.asp. (OCLC's calculations)

43. NCES. 2015. "Table 303.40. Total Fall Enrollment in Degree-Granting Postsecondary Institutions, by Attendance Status, Sex, and Age: Selected Years, 1970 through 2024." National Center for Education Statistics. https://nces.ed.gov/programs/digest/d14/tables/dt14_303.40.asp. (OCLC's calculations)

44. William J. Hussar and Tabitha M. Bailey. 2017. "Projections of Education Statistics to 2025 Forty-Fourth Edition." Washington, DC. https://nces.ed.gov/pubs2017/2017019.pdf.

45. Martin Van Der Werf and Grant Sabatier. 2009. *The College of 2020: Students*. Chronicle Research Services, a division of the Chronicle of Higher Education, 5. https://www.achsnatl.org/meeting2011/The_College_of_2020-Students.pdf.

46. Ibid., 53.

47. Mitchell L. Stevens. 2015. "Introduction: The Changing Ecology of U.S. Higher Education." In *Remaking College: The Changing Ecology of Higher Education*, edited by Michael W. Kirst and Mitchell L. Stevens, 1–15. Stanford, CA: Stanford University Press.

48. NCES. 2017. "Table 311.15. Number and Percentage of Students Enrolled in Degree-Granting Postsecondary Institutions, by Distance Education Participation, Location of Student, Level of Enrollment, and Control and Level of Institution: Fall 2014 and Fall 2015." National Center for Education Statistics. https://nces.ed.gov/programs/digest/d16/tables/dt16_311.15.asp?current=yes.

49. Ibid.

50. NCES. 2014. "Table 311.20. Number and Percentage of Undergraduate Students Taking Night, Weekend, or Online Classes, by Selected Characteristics: 2011-12." National Center for Education Statistics. https://nces.ed.gov/programs/digest/d15/tables/dt15_311.20.asp.

51. Ibid.

52. Ibid.

53. Stephanie Ewert and Robert Kominski. 2014. M*easuring Alternative Educational Credentials: 2012*. Household Economic Studies P70-138. United States Census Bureau. https://www2.census.gov/library/publications/2014/demographics/p70-138.pdf.

54. As a consequence of this scoping decision, community colleges are excluded from our study. Community colleges are an important sector and may be the subject of future work exploring the application of our model to a broader share of the US higher education sector.

55. Specifically, we included all institutions with a basic Carnegie Classification from "Baccalaureate Colleges: Diverse Fields" through "Doctoral Universities: Highest Research Activity." The initial project population included 1,536 institutions. For practical purposes, we treated each unique IPEDS indicator as a discrete institution in our analysis.

56. The Carnegie Community Engagement Classification is currently managed by the Swearer Center for Public Service at Brown University. See Brown University. "CUEI: College & University Engagement Initiative." Accessed 27 July 2018. https://www.brown.edu /swearer/carnegie.

57. As of 2015, the IPEDS system includes religious affiliations for 883 colleges and universities. See NCES. 2016. "Table 303.90. Fall Enrollment and Number of Degree-granting Postsecondary Institutions, by Control and Religious Affiliation of Institution: Selected years, 1980 through 2015." In *Digest of Education Statistics.* https://nces.ed.gov/programs/digest /d16/tables/dt16_303.90.asp.

58. We explore the issue of institutional religious identity and academic libraries in a blog post: Rona Stein. 2018. "What's in a Name? More Than Meets the Eye, or IPEDS: On the Religious Identity of US Colleges and Universities." *HangingTogether* (blog), *OCLC Research.* 21 March 2018. http://hangingtogether.org/?p=6588.

59. The scoring formula is also available on the OCLC Research University Futures, Library Futures website: https://www.oclc.org/research/publications/2018/oclcresearch-university-futures -library-futures/supplemental.html.

60. Lists of the top one hundred institutions for Research, Liberal education, and Career-directed education are included as an appendix to this report. These lists include the top one hundred highest scoring institutions in each of these categories, based on our institution typology scoring formula, applied to the 1,506 institutions in the project population.

61. ACRL (Association of College and Research Libraries). 2018. *Standards for Libraries in Higher Education, Approved February 2018.* Chicago, IL: ACRL, A division of the American Library Association. http://www.ala.org/acrl/standards/standardslibraries.

62. It should be noted that the basic Carnegie Classification differentiates between Doctoral Moderate Research, Doctoral Higher Research, and Doctoral Highest Research institutions. Based on our typology, the boundaries between these Carnegie categories appear relatively porous: there are institutions in the Moderate Research category with scores within the range of Higher Research, and institutions within the Higher Research category that score as high as institutions in the Highest Research category.

63. Recall that the Research direction in our typology is restricted to doctoral-level research, as measured by variables in our scoring formula. Therefore, Research scores in the Master's and Baccalaureate institutions (as measured in our typology) do not include things like undergraduate research or honors programs.

64. Due to an apparent coding error, one institution in our 2015 IPEDS dataset (Concordia University-Chicago) was categorized as Special Focus Four Year institution and therefore excluded from these figures. As a result, the total population represented in the tables is N=1,505.

65. Reports of declining doctoral enrollments and growing master's and certificate program enrollment continue to fuel speculation that the university research enterprise is undergoing a fundamental organizational transformation, with private institutions capitalizing on growth in the market for master's degrees and certificates. See, e.g., Hironao Okahana, Keonna Feaster, and Jeff Allum. 2016. *Graduate Enrollment and Degrees: 2005 to 2015.* Washington, DC: Council of Graduate Schools. https://cgsnet.org/ckfinder/userfiles/files /Graduate%20Enrollment%20%20Degrees%20Fall%202015%20Final.pdf.

66. A reader shared with us the sense that efforts to transform teaching and learning are missing from this framework, but in our work to identify library services we did not identify any evidence of this as a library service outside of efforts to enable academic success. Put another way, libraries tend to position any work they are taking on regarding transforming teaching and learning as being in the service of enabling academic success, rather than for their own sake.

67. Of the 581 respondents to our December 2017 survey, 555 (96%) are represented within the population modeled in our typology. Among these institutions, the response rate to survey questions regarding institutional and library directions was 100%.

68. These data suggest that the sample of institutions that responded to the December 2017 survey have a slightly greater Research orientation (and lower Career direction) than the population described by our typology. The average values for the University Futures, Library Futures project population is: 8% Research, 62% Liberal Education; and 30% Career-directed Education.

69. Our use of the term New Traditional is consistent with the definition provided in chapter 2 as it operationalized in our institution typology (described in chapter 3).

70. Membership in the University Professional and Continuing Education Association (UPCEA) is open to accredited, degree-granting higher education institutions. The organization includes more than 300 colleges and universities in the US and its membership is at least partially coextensive with the University Futures, Library Futures project population. However, it was not feasible to isolate institutions within our population without additional effort to reconcile institution names and IPEDS identifiers. This is potentially interesting work for some follow-on research.

71. See University Innovation Alliance: http://www.theuia.org/#about.

72. A useful analysis of student support services and the distinctive needs of New Traditional students is presented in: Amy Belcastro, and Vicki T. Purslow. 2006. "An Integrative Framework: Meeting the Needs of the New-traditional Student." Paper presented at the Faculty Work and the New Academy Meeting of the Association of American Colleges and Universities, Chicago, IL, November 2006. http://files.eric.ed.gov/fulltext/ED495297.pdf.

73. It was not feasible, in the context of this project, to coordinate extensive statistical analysis of library services directions based on the key services framework. Clearly, further analysis to investigate the relationship between institutional education directions, enrollment profile and library services priorities as reflected in the survey findings is an interesting avenue for future research. The survey data set will be deposited in the Inter-university Consortium for Political and Social Research (ICPSR) repository, where Ithaka S+R has published other survey data sets. The core IPEDS data set used to construct the institution typology is available here: Constance Malpas, Roger Schonfeld, Rona Stein, Lorcan Dempsey, and Deanna Marcum. 2018. University Futures, Library Futures. "Data Set and Scoring Formula" (file name: "uflf-typology-031618.xlsx"). Dublin, OH: OCLC Research. https://www.oclc.org/research/publications/2018/oclcresearch-university-futures-library-futures/supplemental.html.

74. See Association of American Colleges & Universities. "Mission Statement." Adopted November 2017. https://www.aacu.org/about/mission.

75. See University Innovation Alliance. "Who We Are." http://www.theuia.org/#about.

76. See, e.g., Christopher Hollister. 2005. "Bringing Information Literacy to Career Services." *Reference Services Review* 33(1): 104-11, https://doi.org/10.1108/00907320510581414; and Yoo-Seong Song. 2009. "Designing Library Services Based on User Needs: New Opportunities to Re-position the Library." Paper presented at the World Library and Information Congress: 75th IFLA General Conference and Assembly, "Libraries Create Futures: Building on Cultural Heritage," Thursday, 27 August 2009, Milan, Italy. https://www.ifla.org/past-wlic/2009/202-song-en.pdf.

77. Connaway, *Improving Practice* (see note 3).

78. Ibid., 3-4, 8-9.

79. Adam L. Murray and Ashley P. Ireland. 2017. "Communicating Library Impact on Retention: A Framework for Developing Reciprocal Value Propositions." *Journal of Library Administration* 57(3): 311-26. https://doi.org/10.1080/01930826.2016.1243425.

80. The growing importance of consortia in enabling academic libraries to scale capacity, innovation and influence is examined in a series of blog posts by Lorcan Dempsey. See "The Powers of Library Consortia 1: How Consortia Scale Capacity, Learning, Innovation and Influence." *Lorcan Dempsey's Weblog, OCLC Research*. 28 February 2018. http://orweblog.oclc.org/the-powers-of-library-consortia-1-how-consortia-scale-capacity-learning-innovation-and-influence/.

81. It is unclear why library directors in our focus-group interview of Colorado academic institutions had more personal anecdotes to share regarding student demographics. Further research might usefully explore the range of incentives and other factors that motivate library administrators to consider student demographics as an input to library services planning. Institution size or a rapidly changing enrollment profile could be important factors here.

82. See, e.g., Jeff Selingo. 2018. "The Third Educational Revolution: Schools Are Moving Toward a Model of Continuous, Lifelong Learning in Order to Meet the Needs of Today's Economy." *The Atlantic*. 22 March 2018. https://www.theatlantic.com/education/archive/2018/03/the-third-education-revolution/556091. A growing number of funding bodies and research centers are focused on the changing educational requirements to maximize workforce readiness, well beyond traditional "vo-tech" and two-year, Associate's granting institutions. Consider for example the research agenda of the Center for Education and the Workforce at Georgetown University, as well as programmatic initiatives at the Lumina Foundation, the Strada Foundation's Institute for the Future of Work, and the Postsecondary Success Program at the Bill & Melinda Gates Foundation.

Acknowledgments

This University Futures, Library Futures project benefited from the participation of many contributors who shared expertise and insights with the project team. The authors of this report are pleased to acknowledge the support of the individuals and institutions named below. Any errors or omissions in the report itself are the sole responsibility of the authors.

We would first like to thank colleagues at the Andrew W. Mellon Foundation, especially Donald J. Waters (Senior Program Officer), for providing financial support for the collaboration between OCLC Research and Ithaka S+R.

In developing the institution typology underpinning this project, OCLC Research consulted with a broad range of collaborators who assisted in reviewing, revising and improving our framework. We would like to extend special thanks to Jen Wells, Senior Program Officer at the Postsecondary Success Program, Bill & Melinda Gates Foundation, for her suggestions and guidance in the early phases of this work. We are equally grateful to Christopher N. Oberg Vice President/COO and Linda Petersen, Director of Research (both of the WASC Senior College and University Commission) for sharing their expert knowledge of higher education institutions in California, which assisted us in fine-tuning the typology. Gwen Evans (Executive Director) and Joanna Voss (Collections Analyst) at OhioLINK helpfully provided us with a set of IPEDS identifiers to assist with profiling and validating our typology for institutions Ohio. Colleagues on the OCLC Sales and Member Relations teams (Don Litner, Maruta Skujina, Rob Favini and Eric Forte) and Market Research (Peggy Gallagher) assisted with evaluating the typology and testing the scoring formula.

We presented a preliminary application of our typology in a session at the OCLC Americas Regional Council meeting in Baltimore, MD, in October 2017. Attendees at the session provided helpful feedback that resulted in improvements in our scoring formula. We also benefited from informal consultations with Rebecca Lubas and Sarah Pickle (Claremont Colleges Library), W. Lee Hisle (Connecticut College Library), Ray Granade (Ouachita Baptist University Library) Celeste Feather and Sharla Lair (LYRASIS), Lisa Hinchliffe (University of Illinois, Urbana-Champaign), and Bryan Alexander. We received helpful feedback from attendees at our conference presentations at CNI (April 2018) and the OhioLINK Library Directors meeting (June 2018).

Several library directors helped us to review the key service areas in draft form and to test the survey instrument. We especially thank David Banush (Tulane University), Mark Dahl (Lewis & Clark College), David Lewis (Indiana University-Purdue University Indianapolis), and Danuta Nitecki (Drexel University), for their thoughtful contributions.

Our OCLC colleague Lynn Silipigni Connaway, Director of Library Trends and User Research, provided expert consultation on the design of our focus groups. Geneva Henry, Dean of Libraries and Academic Innovation at George Washington University graciously provided space for focus group with AAC&U member institutions. Cliff Lynch, Executive Director of CNI, was kind enough to provide us with space for our focus group with UIA library deans and directors.

Bridget Burns, Executive Director of UIA, generously sponsored lunch for the directors at this meeting. Our deepest gratitude goes to the many library directors and consortium executives who participated in our focus group meetings. Those individuals and their institutional affiliations are noted at the bottom of this section.

We thank Lynn Silipigni Connaway (Director of Library Trends and User Research, OCLC), Martin Kurzweil (Director of the Educational Transformation Program at Ithaka S+R), Mark McBride (Library Senior Strategist, State University of New York), and Scott Walter (University Librarian, DePaul University) for reviewing a preliminary draft of this report and sharing thoughtful commentary and feedback. Their input improved and refined the final version.

We would additionally like to thank our OCLC Research colleagues Brian Lavoie (Senior Research Scientist) and Rebecca Bryant (Senior Program Officer) for their thoughtful comments and review of a series of project blog posts. Kendra Morgan (Senior Program Manager) provided expert internal coordination for the project. Erin Schadt (Senior Communications Manager) coordinated editing and production of the final report.

UNIVERSITY FUTURES, LIBRARY FUTURES FOCUS GROUP PARTICIPANTS:

- Alison Armstrong, Associate Director for Research and Education, The Ohio State University

- Dana Bostrom, Executive Director, Orbis Cascade Alliance

- Jeffrey Bullington, Library Director, Adams State University

- Rick Burke, Executive Director, SCELC

- Faye Chadwell, Donald and Delpha Campbell University Librarian and Oregon State University Press Director, Oregon State University

- Stephen Connaghan, University Librarian, Catholic University of America

- Rebecca Crist, Project Manager, Big Ten Academic Alliance (BTAA)

- Nancy Davenport, University Librarian, American University

- Andrea Falcone, Associate Director for Education & Public Services, Auraria Library

- Susan Fliss, Dean of Libraries, Smith College

- Peggy Fry, Interim University Librarian, Georgetown University

- Gayle Gunderson, Library Director, Colorado Christian University

- Jennifer Gunter King, Director of the Library and Knowledge Commons, Hampshire College

- Catherine Hamer, Director of Academic Engagement, University of Texas at Austin

- Geneva Henry, Dean of Libraries and Academic Innovation, George Washington University

- Valerie Horton, Director, Minitex

- Bruce Hulse, Director of Information Services, WRLC

- Selma Jaskowski, Associate Director, Technology Services & Resource Management, University of Central Florida

- Kirsten Leonard, Executive Director, PALNI

- Michael Levine-Clark, Dean and Director of University Libraries, University of Denver

- Steven Mandeville-Gamble, University Librarian, University of California, Riverside

- Beth McNeil, Dean of Library Services, Iowa State University

- Jill Morris, Associate Director, PALCI

- Shawn Nicholson, Associate Director for Digital Information & Systems, Michigan State University

- James O'Donnell, University Librarian, Arizona State University

- Katy O'Neill, Associate Director, Loyola Notre Dame Library

- Rhonda Phillips, Dean of Honors College, and Interim Dean of Purdue Libraries, Purdue University

- Barbara Preece, Director, Loyola Notre Dame Library

- Helen Reed, Dean, University Libraries, University of Northern Colorado

- Mary Roach, Associate Dean, University of Kansas

- Trisha Smith, University Librarian, Trinity Washington University

- Jeff Steely, Dean of Libraries, Georgia State University

- Tyler Walters, Dean of University Libraries, Virginia Tech

- John Zenelis, Dean of Libraries and University Librarian, George Mason University

Appendices

APPENDIX A: University Futures, Library Futures Institution Typology—Segments

University Futures, Library Futures Institution Typology: Segments

Top 100 Research-oriented

Top 100 Liberal Education-oriented

Top 100 Career-oriented

Top 100 New Traditional Enrollment Profile

TOP 100 RESEARCH-ORIENTED

UnitID	Institution Name	Research
166683	Massachusetts Institute of Technology	0.552048
110404	California Institute of Technology	0.550904
201645	Case Western Reserve University	0.531581
243744	Stanford University	0.523209
162928	Johns Hopkins University	0.521199
166027	Harvard University	0.51492
198419	Duke University	0.513811
139755	Georgia Institute of Technology-Main Campus	0.5119
211440	Carnegie Mellon University	0.49769
190576	CUNY Graduate School and University Center	0.494535
144050	University of Chicago	0.493916
195030	University of Rochester	0.488853
190150	Columbia University in the City of New York	0.488816

215062	University of Pennsylvania	0.488119
147767	Northwestern University	0.482465
221999	Vanderbilt University	0.48221
240444	University of Wisconsin-Madison	0.477534
193900	New York University	0.476611
186131	Princeton University	0.47504
131496	Georgetown University	0.474742
139658	Emory University	0.474726
199120	University of North Carolina at Chapel Hill	0.474012
179867	Washington University in St Louis	0.472043
197708	Yeshiva University	0.465932
130794	Yale University	0.465302
170976	University of Michigan-Ann Arbor	0.465123
160755	Tulane University of Louisiana	0.463662
100663	University of Alabama at Birmingham	0.460441
215293	University of Pittsburgh-Pittsburgh Campus	0.45634
236948	University of Washington-Seattle Campus	0.456287
131469	George Washington University	0.456134
174066	University of Minnesota-Twin Cities	0.455493
134130	University of Florida	0.454032
123961	University of Southern California	0.453908
190415	Cornell University	0.452938
227757	Rice University	0.452261
186380	Rutgers University-New Brunswick	0.451371
234076	University of Virginia-Main Campus	0.451299

155317	University of Kansas	0.451108
168148	Tufts University	0.450805
165015	Brandeis University	0.449753
110680	University of California-San Diego	0.448938
199193	North Carolina State University at Raleigh	0.44891
145725	Illinois Institute of Technolog	0.448612
172644	Wayne State University	0.447115
110635	University of California-Berkeley	0.445912
163286	University of Maryland-College Park	0.445717
126614	University of Colorado Boulder	0.444407
233921	Virginia Polytechnic Institute and State University	0.442603
145637	University of Illinois at Urbana-Champaign	0.442563
164988	Boston University	0.440674
137351	University of South Florida-Main Campus	0.438885
104179	University of Arizona	0.438623
228787	The University of Texas at Dallas	0.438302
145600	University of Illinois at Chicago	0.438191
159391	Louisiana State University and Agricultural & Mechanical College	0.438023
110662	University of California-Los Angeles	0.437992
181464	University of Nebraska-Lincoln	0.437639
141574	University of Hawaii at Manoa	0.436982
139959	University of Georgia	0.436411
126818	Colorado State University-Fort Collins	0.435045
228723	Texas A & M University-College Station	0.43493
139940	Georgia State University	0.433425

196088	University at Buffalo	0.431057
110644	University of California-Davis	0.430997
221759	The University of Tennessee-Knoxville	0.430651
152080	University of Notre Dame	0.43028
153658	University of Iowa	0.429816
157289	University of Louisville	0.428481
204796	Ohio State University-Main Campus	0.428335
157085	University of Kentucky	0.427462
217156	Brown University	0.426748
201885	University of Cincinnati-Main Campus	0.425215
228778	The University of Texas at Austin	0.423523
229115	Texas Tech University	0.423237
217882	Clemson University	0.423147
135726	University of Miami	0.423037
234030	Virginia Commonwealth University	0.422601
171100	Michigan State University	0.42236
155399	Kansas State University	0.42105
238032	West Virginia University	0.420691
243780	Purdue University-Main Campus	0.418853
187985	University of New Mexico-Main Campus	0.418848
225511	University of Houston	0.417922
106397	University of Arkansas	0.417742
230764	University of Utah	0.417449
167358	Northeastern University	0.417394
218663	University of South Carolina-Columbia	0.417357

207500	University of Oklahoma-Norman Campus	0.415713
196097	Stony Brook University	0.415201
110653	University of California-Irvine	0.415083
134097	Florida State University	0.414574
232186	George Mason University	0.414487
214777	Pennsylvania State University-Main Campus	0.414124
209542	Oregon State University	0.412368
164924	Boston College	0.412301
130943	University of Delaware	0.411927
178396	University of Missouri-Columbia	0.411851
216339	Temple University	0.409235
110705	University of California-Santa Barbara	0.409209

TOP 100 LIBERAL EDUCATION-ORIENTED

UnitID	Institution Name	Liberal Education
106342	Lyon College	1
116846	American Jewish University	1
121257	Pitzer College	1
455770	Providence Christian College	1
399911	Soka University of America	1
124292	Thomas Aquinas College	1
127653	Naropa University	1
446048	Ave Maria University	1
136950	Rollins College	1
138600	Agnes Scott College	1
145691	Illinois College	1
146427	Knox College	1

245847	Antioch University-Santa Barbara	0.99486
222983	Austin College	0.994849
236328	University of Puget Sound	0.994606
204501	Oberlin College	0.991608
232308	Hollins University	0.99128
121345	Pomona College	0.990099
160977	Bates College	0.990099
161004	Bowdoin College	0.990099
161086	Colby College	0.990099
173902	Macalester College	0.990099
174844	St Olaf College	0.990099
198385	Davidson College	0.990099
210669	Allegheny College	0.990099
21338	Lafayette College	0.990099
197133	Vassar College	0.990091
128902	Connecticut College	0.990066
191630	Hobart William Smith Colleges	0.990057
195526	Skidmore College	0.990051
107080	Hendrix College	0.989933
130590	Trinity College	0.989841
150455	Earlham College	0.989501
189088	Bard College	0.987676
245883	Antioch University-Seattle	0.986436
126678	Colorado College	0.985944
232681	University of Mary Washington	0.985228

262129	New College of Florida	0.985222
152673	Wabash College	0.985222
164465	Amherst College	0.985222
174251	University of Minnesota-Morris	0.985222
189097	Barnard College	0.985222
212009	Dickinson College	0.985222
216287	Swarthmore College	0.985222
199111	University of North Carolina at Asheville	0.985134
209922	Reed College	0.985106
231712	Christopher Newport University	0.984644
210492	Bryn Athyn College of the New Church	0.983519
210401	Willamette University	0.982636
120254	Occidental College	0.980392

TOP 100 CAREER-ORIENTED

UnitID	Institution Name	Career
460075	California University of Management and Sciences	0.97037
440411	Marlboro College Graduate & Professional Studies	0.934407
115083	Golden Gate University-San Francisco	0.891055
449870	University of the West	0.827033
245892	Antioch University-Midwest	0.790123
220631	Lincoln Memorial University	0.775974
480569	Florida Institute of Technology-Online	0.756869
243832	EDP University of Puerto Rico Inc-San Juan	0.754825
234915	City University of Seattle	0.748207
241386	Caribbean University-Carolina	0.738462
448284	Doane University-Graduate and Professional Studies	0.731061

173328	Concordia University-Saint Paul	0.729488
363916	Caribbean University-Vega Baja	0.723214
100690	Amridge University	0.712264
230630	Stevens-Henager College	0.711111
462354	John Paul the Great Catholic University	0.710174
241720	Colegio Universitario de San Juan	0.70015
103787	American Indian College Inc	0.7
148335	Robert Morris University Illinois	0.698158
206048	Tiffin University	0.6931
238616	Concordia University-Wisconsin	0.690911
181604	College of Saint Mary	0.687094
201964	Ohio Christian University	0.685358
183211	Rivier University	0.685302
190114	Metropolitan College of New York	0.683453
363907	Caribbean University-Ponce	0.680782
438151	Stevens-Henager College	0.679092
228325	Southwestern Assemblies of God University	0.675325
170675	Lawrence Technological University	0.674907
235422	Heritage University	0.672074
243346	Universidad Del Este	0.670253
241377	Caribbean University-Bayamon	0.668691
461236	Georgia Christian University	0.666667
154688	Baker University	0.665665
170806	Madonna University	0.6624
206349	Ursuline College	0.66187

161873	University of Baltimore	0.661126
161518	Saint Joseph's College of Maine	0.657514
212832	Gwynedd Mercy University	0.653815
169479	Davenport University	0.649404
151801	Indiana Wesleyan University-Marion	0.648972
219718	Bethel University	0.644444
217235	Johnson & Wales University-Providence	0.641056
206613	Wright State University-Lake Campus	0.640807
242635	Inter American University of Puerto Rico-Arecibo	0.634123
414823	Johnson & Wales University-North Miami	0.633094
242644	Inter American University of Puerto Rico-Barranquitas	0.63238
241739	Universidad Metropolitana	0.63106
138868	Point University	0.628099
180522	Montana State University-Northern	0.627993
242626	Inter American University of Puerto Rico-Aguadilla	0.62786
219198	Mount Marty College	0.626621
157377	Midway University	0.625442
166948	Mount Ida College	0.624374
242662	Inter American University of Puerto Rico-Ponce	0.62241
164739	Bentley University	0.619944
164492	Anna Maria College	0.61933
450766	LIU Riverhead	0.617811
214634	Pennsylvania State University-Penn State Shenango	0.617534
241100	American University of Puerto Rico	0.616987
433387	Western Governors University	0.616305

215099	Philadelphia University	0.6161
241225	Universidad Central de Bayamon	0.61597
161563	Thomas College	0.614035
241128	American University of Puerto Rico	0.613722
242699	Inter American University of Puerto Rico-Guayama	0.612263
214883	Peirce College	0.609361
206862	Southern Nazarene University	0.608907
169910	Ferris State University	0.60713
460783	Remington College-Heathrow Campus	0.6
239080	Marian University	0.598191
203775	Malone University	0.597336
155900	Southwestern College	0.589748
155520	MidAmerica Nazarene University	0.588067
101189	Faulkner University	0.587289
172334	Spring Arbor University	0.586528
238430	Cardinal Stritch University	0.586466
181093	Grace University	0.58642
116712	John F. Kennedy University	0.586012
226383	Lubbock Christian University	0.584282
125897	Woodbury University	0.583224
178721	Park University	0.583161
242680	Inter American University of Puerto Rico-Fajardo	0.581481
150172	Calumet College of Saint Joseph	0.581197
167394	College of Our Lady of the Elms	0.580694
480198	Warner Pacific College Adult Degree Program	0.580502

164720	Becker College	0.58042
461795	North American University	0.579065
210775	Alvernia University	0.577739
101587	University of West Alabama	0.57517
174862	Crown College	0.573591
243586	Pontifical Catholic University of Puerto Rico-Mayaguez	0.573066
194392	Paul Smiths College of Arts and Science	0.571413
428259	Ottawa University-Milwaukee	0.569507
206835	Oklahoma Wesleyan University	0.564208
219949	Cumberland University	0.56407
226231	LeTourneau University	0.56351
220206	Welch College	0.563218
151786	Marian University	0.563208
204194	Mount Vernon Nazarene University	0.562339

TOP 100 NEW TRADITIONAL ENROLLMENT PROFILE

UnitID	Institution Name	New Traditional
480134	Elizabethtown College School of Continuing and Professional Studies	0.992
428259	Ottawa University-Milwaukee	0.980754
196680	Excelsior College	0.978022
105367	Ottawa University-Phoenix	0.969743
454582	Ottawa University-Online	0.966265
437325	Linfield College-Online and Continuing Education	0.964803
187046	Thomas Edison State University	0.96446
222628	Amberton University	0.959047
155636	Ottawa University-Kansas City	0.950933
475200	Whitworth University-Adult Degree Programs	0.923876

128780	Charter Oak State College	0.923671
457697	City Vision University	0.91741
476975	Colorado State University-Global Campus	0.912015
163204	University of Maryland-University College	0.904498
214883	Peirce College	0.898331
479956	Pennsylvania State University-World Campus	0.897715
100690	Amridge University	0.895395
135610	Trinity International University-Florida	0.885589
262086	Brandman University	0.873763
480569	Florida Institute of Technology-Online	0.873264
440411	Marlboro College Graduate & Professional Studies	0.87031
209108	Marylhurst University	0.868493
448804	The Robert B Miller College	0.858631
483036	Texas A & M University-Central Texas	0.854586
229780	Wayland Baptist University	0.840946
196264	SUNY Empire State College	0.838128
179894	Webster University	0.833649
175421	Belhaven University	0.831861
115083	Golden Gate University-San Francisco	0.827926
183026	Southern New Hampshire University	0.825497
144351	Concordia University-Chicago	0.824158
147536	National Louis University	0.823724
231651	Regent University	0.819256
188182	University of the Southwest	0.818525
178721	Park University	0.817853

151810	Martin University	0.816284
482705	Northeastern University Professional Advancement Network	0.810918
135081	Keiser University-Ft Lauderdale	0.810392
450766	LIU Riverhead	0.808955
245892	Antioch University-Midwest	0.806216
459727	Touro University Worldwide	0.805776
234915	City University of Seattle	0.802718
206279	Union Institute & University	0.802223
170842	Marygrove College	0.802086
483124	Arizona State University-Skysong	0.798239
119605	National University	0.792218
232557	Liberty University	0.791435
177065	Columbia College	0.789837
169479	Davenport University	0.787276
161217	University of Maine at Augusta	0.787115
102632	University of Alaska Southeast	0.785069
165167	Cambridge College	0.78349
174020	Metropolitan State University	0.783189
116712	John F. Kennedy University	0.782409
367884	Hodges University	0.77682
183257	Granite State College	0.773757
163578	Notre Dame of Maryland University	0.772884
131113	Wilmington University	0.76786
155900	Southwestern College	0.767383
100812	Athens State University	0.766893

148584	University of St Francis	0.76528
190576	CUNY Graduate School and University Center	0.764497
199069	University of Mount Olive	0.76056
225502	University of Houston-Victoria	0.758498
178059	Maryville University of Saint Louis	0.756425
460783	Remington College-Heathrow Campus	0.756032
243832	EDP University of Puerto Rico Inc-San Juan	0.754208
448309	Shorter University-College of Adult & Professional Programs	0.753798
131399	University of the District of Columbia	0.751597
136215	Nova Southeastern University	0.747932
201964	Ohio Christian University	0.746075
448284	Doane University-Graduate and Professional Studies	0.737379
145336	Governors State University	0.735948
137032	Saint Leo University	0.731809
245883	Antioch University-Seattle	0.731196
156541	University of the Cumberlands	0.728357
180814	Bellevue University	0.725061
131876	Trinity Washington University	0.724813
206835	Oklahoma Wesleyan University	0.722796
363907	Caribbean University-Ponce	0.720704
193645	The College of New Rochelle	0.719821
190114	Metropolitan College of New York	0.71979
144005	Chicago State University	0.718847
241386	Caribbean University-Carolina	0.718355
225432	University of Houston-Downtown	0.717016

157377	Midway University	0.716832
142522	Brigham Young University-Idaho	0.716658
363916	Caribbean University-Vega Baja	0.716104
139199	Brenau University	0.715429
141167	Thomas University	0.714807
126669	Colorado Christian University	0.711968
161518	Saint Joseph's College of Maine	0.710418
441900	Nevada State College	0.709956
238980	Lakeland University	0.708154
152381	Saint Mary-of-the-Woods College	0.705527
160630	Southern University at New Orleans	0.705132
414878	Trine University-Regional/Non-Traditional Campuses	0.704638
187897	New Mexico Highlands University	0.703653
188304	Western New Mexico University	0.703528
110316	California Institute of Integral Studies	0.703149

Appendix B: Survey Instrument with Response Rates

To access the entire dataset of responses, visit oc.lc/uflf-report.

For how many years have you been the library director or dean at [Institution Name]?

- Less than 2 years
- 2-5 years
- 6-10 years
- 11-15 years
- More than 15 years

Responses: 735

Thinking about [Institution Name], how would you describe the balance of research, liberal education, and career-focused educational activity? A rough estimate is perfectly acceptable; we are looking for your general impression of how educational activity is distributed across these three areas. Please ensure that the percentages total 100%.

- Research: Graduate and postgraduate research in the sciences and humanities; programs conferring doctoral degrees
- Liberal education: Interdisciplinary baccalaureate education providing broad exposure to the arts and sciences
- Career focus: Baccalaureate, master's and non-degree certificate programs in specific professional fields, e.g. business management, criminal justice, education, health care

Responses: 693

Thinking about your library and any other libraries at [Institution Name], how would you describe the balance of services supporting research, liberal education, and career-focused educational activity? A rough estimate is perfectly acceptable; we are looking for your general impression of how institutional activity is distributed across these three areas. Please ensure that the percentages total 100%.

- Research: Graduate and postgraduate research in the sciences and humanities; programs conferring doctoral degrees
- Liberal education: Interdisciplinary baccalaureate education providing broad exposure to the arts and sciences
- Career focus: Baccalaureate, master's and non-degree certificate programs in specific professional fields, e.g. business management, criminal justice, education, health care

Responses: 693

Thinking about [Institution Name], how would you estimate the balance of "Residential" compared to "Flexible/convenience" educational programs that it offers? "Residential" is defined as principally on-campus and/or full-time and "Flexible/convenience" is defined as

principally online and/or part-time. (Using a scale of 1 to 100 where 1=Residential (principally on-campus and/or full-time) and 100=Flexible/convenience (principally online and/or part-time)).

Responses: 655

1					25					50					75					100

Residential (principally on-campus and/or full-time)

Flexible/ convenience (principally online and/or part-time)

Thinking about your library and any other libraries at [Institution Name], how would you estimate the balance of services you offer in support of "Residential" compared to "Flexible/ convenience" educational programs? "Residential" is defined as principally on-campus and/or full-time and "Flexible/convenience" is defined as principally online and/or part-time. (Using a scale of 1 to 100 where 1=Residential (principally on-campus and/or full-time) and 100=Flexible/ convenience (principally online and/or part-time)).

Responses: 633

1					25					50					75					100

Residential (principally on-campus and/or full-time)

Flexible/ convenience (principally online and/or part-time)

For each key service area identified below, please estimate the approximate share of resources your library currently devotes to each. Resources should include staffing, materials budget, space, other direct expenses, charged overhead, etc.—in other words, your entire budget, which includes all back-office functions. Please ensure that the total equals 100%—we understand it will be necessary to approximate.

- Convene Campus Community: Provide spaces and facilitate programs that for the community broadly or specific sub-populations to generate engagement, outreach, and inclusion

- Enable Academic Success: Support instruction, facilitate learning, improve information literacy, and/or maximize retention, progression, graduation, and later life success

- Facilitate Information Access: Enable discovery and usage of information resources of any format or ownership; provide for preservation of general collections

- Foster Scholarship and Creation: Deliver expertise, assistance, tools, and services that support research and creative work

- Include and Support Off-Campus Users: Provide equitable access for part-time students, distance & online learners, and other principally off-campus/non-campus/remote users

- Preserve and Promote Unique Collections: Ensure the long-term stewardship of rare materials & special collections and maximize their usage

- Provide Study Space: Provide physical spaces for academic collaboration, quiet study, and technology-enhanced instruction and/or learning

- Showcase Scholarly Expertise: Promote research excellence and subject matter expertise of scholars and other affiliates; includes repository activities for open access preprint materials

- Transform Scholarly Publishing: Drive towards modernized formats, revamped business models, and reduced market concentration

Responses: 645

To maximize the fit between library service offerings and the priorities of [Institution Name], how would you allocate resources across these same key service areas?

- Convene Campus Community: Provide spaces and facilitate programs that for the community broadly or specific sub-populations to generate engagement, outreach, and inclusion

- Enable Academic Success: Support instruction, facilitate learning, improve information literacy, and/or maximize retention, progression, graduation, and later life success

- Facilitate Information Access: Enable discovery and usage of information resources of any format or ownership; provide for preservation of general collections

- Foster Scholarship and Creation: Deliver expertise, assistance, tools, and services that support research and creative work

- Include and Support Off-Campus Users: Provide equitable access for part-time students, distance & online learners, and other principally off-campus/non-campus/remote users

- Preserve and Promote Unique Collections: Ensure the long-term stewardship of rare materials & special collections and maximize their usage

- Provide Study Space: Provide physical spaces for academic collaboration, quiet study, and technology-enhanced instruction and/or learning

- Showcase Scholarly Expertise: Promote research excellence and subject matter expertise of scholars and other affiliates; includes repository activities for open access preprint materials

- Transform Scholarly Publishing: Drive towards modernized formats, revamped business models, and reduced market concentration

Responses: 458

Looking ahead five years, how do you anticipate you will allocate resources across these same key service areas?

- Convene Campus Community: Provide spaces and facilitate programs that for the community broadly or specific sub-populations to generate engagement, outreach, and inclusion

- Enable Academic Success: Support instruction, facilitate learning, improve information literacy, and/or maximize retention, progression, graduation, and later life success

- Facilitate Information Access: Enable discovery and usage of information resources of any format or ownership; provide for preservation of general collections

- Foster Scholarship and Creation: Deliver expertise, assistance, tools, and services that support research and creative work
- Include and Support Off-Campus Users: Provide equitable access for part-time students, distance & online learners, and other principally off-campus/non-campus/remote users
- Preserve and Promote Unique Collections: Ensure the long-term stewardship of rare materials & special collections and maximize their usage
- Provide Study Space: Provide physical spaces for academic collaboration, quiet study, and technology-enhanced instruction and/or learning
- Showcase Scholarly Expertise: Promote research excellence and subject matter expertise of scholars and other affiliates; includes repository activities for open access preprint materials
- Transform Scholarly Publishing: Drive towards modernized formats, revamped business models, and reduced market concentration

Responses: 449

What was your library's FY2012 annual budget (including personnel, collections, and all other expenditures)?

Responses: 531

What is your library's FY2017 annual budget (including personnel, collections, and all other expenditures)?

Responses: 542

For how many years have you been in the library field/profession?

Responses: 582

For how many years have you been in a library leadership role?

Responses: 583

For more information on the University Futures,
Library Futures project, visit **oc.lc/research**.

ITHAKA S·R

ISBN: 978-1-55653-076-0
DOI: 10.25333/WS5K-DD86

RM-PR-216091-WWAE 1810